Aspects of History

Issue 12

Table of Contents

ISSUE 12

From the Editor

Welcome to October's issue of Aspects of History, which, in the period between our previous issue has seen historic events. Now that word 'historic' is often misused, but in Britain, we've seen both our head of state, Queen Elizabeth II, and Prime Minister replaced in a seamless transition of power. The Queen reigned over a nation that emerged from the Second World War into a period of decolonisation, and an explosion of cultural creativity from the 1960s, and all the while as a model of stoicism. She also dealt with 15 Prime Ministers of varying quality from Winston Churchill to the present incumbent. The fact that the state can deal with two major constitutional changes in as many days, without violence, is certainly remarkable. One only has to look over the Atlantic Ocean and to the events at the Capitol in January 2021 to see that there are democratic countries that have struggled with such a transition.

In 1660 the Restoration occurred seamlessly, in no small part thanks to General Monck as Charles II reclaimed the throne taken from his father. Within months, the Indemnity and Oblivion Act was passed, which on the one hand was an olive branch to Parliamentarians, but on the other was certainly vengeance against those regicides responsible for Charles I's execution. Robert Harris has written a thrilling novel based around that Act, and the consequences of it, and he chatted with me about that incredible period of British history.

The recent Ukrainian gains at the Russians' expense are to be welcomed, and we have a number of contributions from authors with deep knowledge of the nation Churchill described as 'a riddle, wrapped in a mystery, inside an enigma.' Where better than to try to understand Russia but from Rodric Braithwaite, Katie Stallard and Max Hastings – respectively an ambassador, journalist and historian.

This issue's Historical Hero is that most tragic of figures from the Tudor period, Mary Queen of Scots. A woman who made some dreadful decisions, but was mother to King James I and VI, and who Elizabeth II can trace her lineage back to.

The Aspects of History Podcast continues – I'd encourage you to listen. Some of the interviews in this issue have more extended turnouts where you can delve into a subject in more detail. We've also had discussions with Royal historian Dr Tessa Dunlop, Miranda Malins on Oliver Cromwell, Helen Fry on Thomas Kendrick the Spymaster, and Barney White-Spunner on the Partition of India. I also chat with Giles Milton on the AoH Book Club – the terrible events at Smyrna in 1922. You'll find the podcast in all the usual places.

We continue to offer Author Platforms on our website for historians, historical novelists, academics, and students to write about their books and history in an ongoing way. In addition, we can provide publishing and promotional services to assist authors and would-be authors – from pitch to publication and beyond. If you are a member of an historical society or creative writing group, then do get in touch.

If you are interested in finding out more, please visit our website at aspectsofhistory.com, follow us on Twitter @aspectshistory, or email me at editor@aspectsofhistory.com. I am always happy to hear from readers and writers alike. This continues to be as much your magazine as ours.

Oliver Webb Carter

Editor & Co-Founder

ASPECTS OF HISTORY

Editor: Oliver Webb-Carter
Advisory Board: Saul David, Richard Foreman, Roger Moorhouse,
Antonia Senior
Designer: Nick Kevern
Web Designer: Luke Rogers
Production Assistant: Tara Flynn
Social Media: Andrew Critchell

A Divided Kingdom: Robert Harris on his new novel, Act of Oblivion

Robert Harris is the bestselling author of many novels including *Fatherland*, *The Ghost* and *Munich*. He's now turned to the 17th century in his latest book, Act of Oblivion. Set in the aftermath of the restoration, it is the story of two men, Edward Whalley and William Goffe, as they flee from the wrath of King Charles II and our editor met him recently to discuss it.

In preparation for my meeting with Robert Harris (of course I'd read his latest novel, *Act of Oblivion*), I read a number of interviews and listened to his Desert Island Discs with Kirsty Young. 12 years old now, it is a fascinating and enlightening episode, and gave an insight into a man who began his career at the BBC. In it he mentioned 'politics is the drama of life'. Harris was The Observer's Political Editor from 1987. Born to working class parents in 1957, he read English at Cambridge, and after Newsnight and Panorama at the BBC he moved to The Observer in 1987. He is now a hugely successful author and has been since his first, Fatherland, was published in 1992 to great acclaim. Having written about ancient Rome, the 1930s, and the Second World War, this is his first foray into the 1600s, but what a century for dramatic politics, with civil war, regicide, republic, restoration and revolution.

As regular readers of the magazine will know, we've had a whole host of authors write for us on the 17th century. From Miranda Malins and her fiction centring on the Cromwell family, to non-fiction from Leanda de Lisle and Clare Jackson, recent winner of the Wolfson Prize. It's no wonder Harris sees this century as attractive for a novelist, but was it that, or the two regicides of the story, Colonels Whalley and Goffe that led him to Act of Oblivion?

"Well, I was attracted because I saw, I think, on Twitter, just a line saying, the greatest manhunt of the 17th century. The concept of the two things together caught my interest. And, of course, it turned out to be the hunt for the men who signed King Charles I's death warrant and sat as judges at his trial. And I read a bit about it and I thought, would it be great to invent the Manhunter? Because we don't know who it was, but someone must have organised [it]. So, I […] invented a Sub-Committee of the Privy Council and a clerk to the Sub-Committee and so on. So that was my starting point, to create the man on their trail and why he would be so determined. And then I looked at the Regicides and it was obvious to me that the two most interesting for my purposes would be Whalley and Goffe. They were father-in-law and son-in-law. The old man, Whalley, who was 60, was Cromwell's cousin, and was close to him, and they fled to America and were hunted across America for years. And I just thought that this

1

would be a great story. It was as simple as that. I have always been interested in the English Civil War, but been deterred from writing a novel about it simply because of its complexity."

Whalley and Goffe, the two regicides of the novel, on the run in America, are very different. Edward 'Ned' Whalley has a sense of humour, William Goffe does not, though both are, unsurprisingly, religious. I wonder how close that was to reality? Harris' answer surprises me, as he's uncovered something about Goffe hitherto unknown.

"Well, obviously, I researched and read everything that is available about them and indeed I found out new facts about them, as far as I can see, that people didn't know before. For instance, the precise date of Goffe's birth, which is about seven years after most estimates. He was 20 years younger than his father-in-law; and Whalley, his wife, [I found] her real name. I think I'm probably the first to track that down, but there are letters from them to Oliver Cromwell's Chief Secretary, that give us some insight into their characters.

"…there are letters between Goffe, the son-in-law and his wife back in England. And these do give you a flavour of their character. And it is true that Whalley was, I think, a far more confident man. He was from a background of gentry…although they've fallen on hard times…He was considered a bit of a dandy…definitely a political moderate. For instance, he urged moderation on Cromwell when he set off on his expedition to Ireland. And mercifully, neither of the two men went on that expedition. And Goffe, we know from the Putney Debates, was fiery, almost a Fifth Monarchist [who] believed that Christ would return to earth in 1666. And he was a political extremist and very much against any negotiations with the King. And curiously, this hasn't really been touched on by other writers about the Regicides. Whalley, for about nine months, was the King's jailer. When he was in the army's hands, he was in charge of him. He seems to become quite close to Charles as well as being close to Cromwell. So, there were lots of straws that I could use to build the bricks of the characters."

Mention of Charles I pleases me, because I had been meaning to ask Harris of what his view of the monarch was, after all he is a sympathetic figure in the book.

"Well, until I really got into writing the novel, I hadn't appreciated how clever he was at the trial and how the Regicides, when they were caught, hanged, drawn and quartered, almost to a man, I think, died very bravely, died in the certainty that they were right. Charles I, on the scaffold, died very bravely in the certainty that he was right as well, and I found that the mirror image of the two in that certainty was interesting. I did have some sympathy for him. I've always regarded myself rather lazily, assumed that I would be a Roundhead. But having spent a lot of time in the company of these Puritan colonels, I decided that probably I'm one of nature's Cavaliers. Actually. It was technically very difficult. It's technically easier, frankly, to write about King Charles I than it is to write about two Puritan colonels on the run. There were many times when I thought, what on earth have I done? What sort of task have I set myself here to make these figures comprehensible and sympathetic to a reader?"

We've mentioned Cromwell, and like Charles I, there have been revisionist histories recently, not least Providence Lost by Paul Lay. I'm interested to understand Harris' view of a man who has been incredibly divisive, and not just to Irishmen and women.

"Well, he was a force of nature and he was a great man. His achievement is staggering: to have gone from a moderately well-off farmer and […] backbench MP with, as far as we know, no military training whatsoever, to found and lead what became probably the greatest army in the world and to completely destroy the professional soldiers on the other side. He was inspirational, brilliant and a curious mixture of qualities of ruthlessness and violence, and compassion and sentiment, and who had the most marvellous way with language.

"The thing you...can never sort out with Cromwell is how much of the religion is genuine. I think almost all of it, but how much of it is also delusional or self-interest? And how ambitious was he? I think there's little doubt when you look at it, that he was extremely ambitious and saw that there was a route opening up for him to take absolute power. He obviously revelled in power, but one of the reasons he was able to was because even his enemies grudgingly accepted that Cromwell was the biggest man in the country. Once the King was dead and his son was in exile, there was only Cromwell. As long as Cromwell was on the scene, more or less, the show could hold together. The Commonwealth moment, of course, he was removed then there wasn't anyone with his stature. I think we can debate endlessly because the evidence is inconclusive. He was a very secretive man, I think, in terms of what was going on. In his head and what he was planning. So we can debate endlessly whether he was a good thing or a bad thing, to use the cliché, but sure as hell he was a thing. One of the most remarkable men that this country has ever produced..."

All these descriptions of Cromwell, Charles I, Whalley and Goffe – would suggest this is a male dominated novel, but that isn't the case. Harris has managed to capture the female experience, and its one that isn't mute in the background. Women underwent much suffering, not least in childbirth, but were frequently the main figure of the family during the Civil War as men went off to fight.

"Yes, so many of the characters which I put in the book were on their second wife, and in almost all cases, the first wife had died in childbirth. And it must have been hellish. In fact, when they are discussing the Register, the possibility, the prospect of hanging, drawing and quartering, the notion was that actually any ordinary woman probably had gone through equivalent pain and goes through it every year, practically, and a lot of them die at the end of it. So, yes, women are the kind of heroes, in a way. They hold the families together when the men are on the run and they are pragmatic and sensible. They don't have political power and obviously they're not soldiers, but they are really crucial. And there are a couple of very strong women in the book. And I liked that, the fact that that was realistic, that I wasn't writing some kind of kick ass 17th century maiden. I hate that in contemporary fiction, you've now got to make the women all like men and killing people and the rest of it. They were very formidable, but in a different way and a more impressive plan somewhere."

We're coming to the end of the interview, and I'm intrigued to understand whether Harris thinks the execution Charles I was actually good for England, and later the United Kingdom, in the long run? After all, a line in the sand had been drawn between Parliament and the Crown. It's one that Sovereigns have largely respected since. Our most recent monarch, Elizabeth II, exemplified respect for the constitutional duties of the monarch.

"I think that they were right to that extent. He had to be got rid of. Whether a trial was the right way, I don't know, because, of course, like many political leaders, Charles was able to use [it] as a platform and he had the best of it. In the end they had to try him in absentia because every time they brought him out, he would say, 'Before we go any further, under what law am I being tried?' Of course, they couldn't really answer this. His behaviour at the trial and the fact that this became a pamphlet and was read everywhere…were propaganda victories for him. There is a case that the army would have been far better to have just bumped him off whilst he was trying to escape, which he repeatedly did try to [do]…I think that by that time Cromwell was determined to, as he said, cut off the King's head with [the] crown still upon it. To dispense with this figure who had, as far as they were concerned, an impediment both to peace and to the relationship between people and God."

Before we do end it, I have the most important question of all. Is Harris a Roundhead or a Cavalier?

"Well, obviously I'm drawn to the radicalism of giving everyone their destiny… so, as a 21st century person, of course, I find all those ideas very attractive. What I don't find attractive and what I find alienating is the puritanism of the army, which is remarkably similar in some respects to ISIS or Al Qaeda. It's a kind of Protestant Taliban smashing up images, destroying and desecrating things they don't believe in, forbidding, suppressing music and services, festivals, theatre, entertainment. That rigidity, that ruthlessness, I find distinctly unappealing. But I kind of accept what Carlyle wrote. I must be one of the very few people in recent years has read Carlyle [Oliver Cromwell's Letters and Speeches: with Elucidations] and he thinks that it was the one time in British history when the greatest people were in charge, when this was the most noble, the most extraordinary thought-through experiment and a new way of living…so when I say I'm a Cavalier, I suppose what I mean by that [is that I] like a drink and a song and going to the theatre and I find this crazy, millennial, Christ will return in 1666, leaves me completely cold."

Robert Harris is the bestselling novelist and author of *Act of Oblivion*. You can listen to a full interview with Robert on the Aspects of History Podcast.

First in, Last Out: US Marines in the Pacific, by Saul David

On August 12, 1942, five days after the 19,000-strong 1st Marine Division had landed unopposed on Guadalcanal in the British Solomon Islands, the first American ground offensive of the war, Sergeant Jim McEnery came upon the aftermath of a slaughter of US Marines who had walked blindly into an ambush. Not satisfied with mere killing, the Japanese had hacked the Americans to pieces. Random body parts littered the river bank. "The first thing I saw," recalled Sergeant Jim McEnery, "was the severed head of a marine… the head was. Moving back and forth in the water and looked like it was alive. Then I realised it was just bobbing in the small waves lapping at the shore."

For most of these Americans, this was their first taste of war. "Why would anyone do this?" a bewildered 17-year-old asked. "Wasn't killing them enough?"

Another sergeant, Thurman Miller, wrote: "That day on the Matanikau," wrote Sergeant Thurman Miller, "we beheld all the horrors of war, all the degrees of degradation to which the human race could descend. We were hardened by much training, and our reflexes were sudden, our minds alert, but now our killing potential was amplified. A second ingredient, hatred, had been added. What kind of warfare was this?"

They were all members of K Company, 3/5 Marines, better known by their nickname 'Devil Dogs' (supposedly given to them by their awed German opponents after the vicious Battle of Belleau Wood in 1918). They were among the first units in and the last out. As Allied forces edged ever closer to Japan, they fought at Guadalcanal, Cape Gloucester, Peleliu and Okinawa. They were preparing to invade the Japanese mainland when the atom bomb brought the war to a sudden and unexpected close.

Some were pre-war regulars, but most of the Devil Dogs had volunteered or were drafted after the Japanese attack on Pearl Harbor in December 1941. They were a cross-section of American society, and included New England college boys, dirt-poor hicks from West Virginia, and confidence tricksters from New York City. Their only commonality was suffering. "Up there, on the line, with nothing between us and the enemy but space (and precious little of that)," wrote one veteran, "we'd forged a bond that time would never erase. We were brothers. I left with a sense of loss and sadness, but K/3/5 will always be a part of me."

Guadalcanal

K Company's first campaign was Operation Watchtower, the attempt to recapture the island of Guadalcanal as a means of protecting Australia and New Zealand, and beginning the roll-back of recent Japanese advances in the Pacific. With minimal preparation and inadequate intelligence, the vanguard of the 1st Marine Division landed on the north coast of Guadalcanal on 7 August 1942. K Company was in the first wave, hurrying up the beach towards the jungle's edge. Among them was 23-year-old Sergeant Thurman Miller, 22, one of 16 siblings born into grinding poverty in Otsego, West Virginia. "There we waited," recalled Miller, "for incoming fire that never came. There were no bullets, no sound except the men behind us as we ran toward the jungle. We had caught the enemy off guard."

The main objective was to capture an airfield the Japanese were in the process of constructing a few miles to the west. This was achieved bloodlessly a day later after Japanese naval construction troops had withdrawn further west. But a disastrous naval defeat during the night of 8/9 August – when four US Navy heavy cruisers were sunk in the Sealark Channel (henceforth known as Iron Bottom Sound) – meant the withdrawal of all supply ships, leaving the Marines to fend for themselves.

As well as battling the harsh tropical climate, inadequate supplies, and chronic malaria and dysentery, the Marines had to contend with an enemy that refused to surrender and did not take prisoners.

During their time on Guadalcanal, K Company took part in a number of desperate actions to defend the airfield. By early November, however, they were ready to take the offensive across the nearby Matanikau River. Killed during a successful bayonet attack on an enemy strong point, Corporal Weldon DeLong of K Company was awarded a posthumous Navy Cross, the highest gallantry award a Marine could be given after the Medal of Honor. His body was found by Sergeant Jim McEnery, 22, a "scrappy kind of kid" who never "dodged a challenge or ducked a fight" from an Irish blue-collar neighbourhood in South Brooklyn, New York. "He was lying in a puddle of blood," wrote McEnery, "with his eyes wide open and his pistol still in his hand. The bullet had gone straight through his heart. He was as dead as a man could get."

The officer leading the attack was the commander of I Company, Captain Erskine Wells. Also awarded the Navy Cross, Wells' valour that day was in stark contrast to the behaviour of K Company's skipper, Captain Lawrence Patterson, who refused to venture further forward than his command post. Patterson was sacked soon after, but it was not until the arrival of Captain Andy Haldane, after the Guadalcanal campaign, that K Company got the skipper it deserved.

By the time the Devil Dogs left Guadalcanal on 9 December, after a brutal four-month campaign, they were a rag-tag bunch, "dressed in green dungarees or dirty khaki, often with limbs protruding from shirts chopped back to the shoulders, trousers clipped at the knees, or sleeves and pant legs that ended in fringes of tatters". But they and the rest of the 1st Marine

Division had broken the back of the enemy's resistance. When the Japanese finally withdrew, two months later, they left behind the corpses of 30,000 soldiers, sailors and airmen. Total American fatalities were 7,100, including 1,769 Marines.

Guadalcanal, concluded Japanese commander Major General Kawaguchi, was the "graveyard of the Japanese army". For US Army Chief of Staff General Marshall, it marked the "turning point in the Pacific" thanks to "the resolute defence of these Marines and the desperate gallantry of our naval task forces".

New Britain

There was now a pause of almost a year as the Devil Dogs got some R & R at Melbourne in Australia, replenished their numbers and prepared for their next campaign on the 370-mile long island of New Britain in the Bismarck Archipelago. Led since the previous spring by the inspirational Captain Andrew "Ack-Ack" Haldane – a football star at Bowdoin University who had earned his spurs as a machine-gunner on Guadalcanal – K Company landed at Cape Gloucester, on the western tip of New Britain, on New Year's Day, 1944. It was given the task of advancing through a hot and humid 'rain forest' – where some trees rose 200 feet and vines were as thick as a man's arm – to capture Aogiri Ridge, a "jungle rise hidden by dense foliage". All along the crest of the ridge, and sprinkled over its steep face, the Japanese had constructed "an elaborate network of camouflaged bunkers and machine gun emplacements".

K Company attacked on 8 and 9 January, eventually reaching a point just below the crest of the ridge where they dug in. To protect this position, a 37mm anti-tank gun was manhandled up the slope by volunteers who included the 30-year-old battalion commander, Lieutenant Colonel "Silent Lew" Walt, and Private First Class R. V. Burgin of the Mortar Section. Burgin, a 20-year-old farmboy from Jewett, Texas, who had joined K Company as a replacement in Australia, remembered: "We took turns, five or six of us at a time, wrestling that rascal up the hill in the mid. I pushed part of the way, slipping and sliding, vines snatching at my boots. As a reward they let me fire it."

That night the Japanese launched no few than five "Banzai" attacks to recapture the ridge. One was stopped just yards from the anti-tank gun; another reached the Company Command Post where Captain Andy Haldane, the much-admired company commander, saved a sergeant by shooting two Japanese with his carbine. During the fifth and final charge, Walt called down defensive artillery fire almost on to K Company's position, wiping out the Japanese assault but also killing some of his own men. As dawn broke, glassy eyed and exhausted Marines moved forward to secure the whole ridge – later dubbed "Walt's Ridge" - mopping up pockets of resistance as they went.

The capture of the ridge was one of the great feats of the Pacific War. Awarded the Navy Cross for his part in the battle, Walt acknowledged the role played by K Company. "There has never been," he wrote, "a better group of fighters." This was confirmed by the award of an unusually high number of gallantry medals to K Company men, including a Silver Star for

Captain Haldane. But the victory came at a high cost. Among the fatalities were all three rifle platoon commanders. One of them, Bill Reckus, was awarded a posthumous Navy Cross

The battle tore the heart out of K Company. It had landed with six officers and 190 men. Ten days later, thanks to illness and battle casualties, it was down to just two officers and eighty-eight men.

Pavuvu

Evacuated from New Britain in early May, the Devil Dogs were shipped to Pavuvu in the Russell Islands, 'a wasteland of oozy mud littered with millions of coconuts and besieged by armes of rats and land crabs". There they were joined by 20-year-old replacement Eugene B. Sledge from Mobile, Alabama, who would go on to write With the Old Breed, arguably the finest memoir of the Pacific War.

Peleliu

Sledge received his baptism of fire in September 1944 on Peleliu, in the Palau Islands, a campaign described by one Devil Dog as "thirty days of the meanest, around-the-clock slaughter that desperate men can inflict on each other".

One night a soldier started yelling hysterically. Worried he would reveal their position, his comrades tried to comfort him, then gave him morphine, then punched him. Nothing worked. Finally, they hit him a little too hard with a shovel and killed him. Sledge wrote of the "agony and distress etched on the strong faces" of the men who "had done what any of us would have had to do under the circumstances".

Wary of the Japanese practice of resisting even when wounded, the Devil Dogs rarely took prisoners. Some collected the enemy's gold teeth. A lieutenant enjoyed urinating in the mouths of Japanese corpses. One marine proudly showed off a cherished souvenir – the desiccated hand of a Japanese soldier, hacked off and carefully dried in the sun. "The war," wrote Sledge, "had gotten to my friend; he had lost (briefly, I hoped) all his sensitivity. He was a twentieth-century savage now, mild mannered though he still was. I shuddered to think that I might do the same thing if the war went on and on."

Yet at other times they were capable of great acts of kindness. One marine cradled the head of his comrade as he slowly died. Another made a bracelet of shells for his mother. "I hope," he wrote to her, "because those dainty little shells came from such a dreadful place, that you won't fail to see their beauty and know [that] they show you were in my mind continuously."

Towards the end of their deployment on Peleliu, the Devil Dogs lost their hugely popular company commander, Andy Haldane, when he was shot by a Japanese sniper as he led a small patrol to an Observation Post. Sledge was 'stunned and sickened' by the news. He wrote later:

Captain Andy Haldane wasn't an idol. He was human. But he commanded our destinies under the most trying conditions with the utmost compassion. We knew he could never be replaced. He was the finest Marine officer I ever knew. The loss of many close friends grieved me deeply... But to all of us the loss of our company commander at Peleliu was like losing a parent we depended upon for security – not our physical security, because we knew that was a commodity beyond our reach in combat, but our mental security

In late October, with the task force commander having declared an end to 'assault' operations on the island, the Devil Dogs returned to Pavuvu to prepare for their next assignment. Before leaving, the surviving two officers and 83 men of K Company – out of an original complement of 235, a casualty rate of 64 per cent – assembled for a picture on the beach. It is one of the most famous and poignant of the Pacific War.

Okinawa

The Devil Dogs' final campaign – though they did not know it at the time – was to capture the 70-mile long island of Okinawa, the most southerly of Japan's prefectures, in the spring of 1945. Having invaded on 1 April, it took the US Tenth Army almost three months to subdue the 100,000 Japanese defenders who had turned "several jagged lines of ridges and rocky escarpments" in the centre of the island into "formidable nests of interlocking pillboxes and firing positions". All were "connected by a network of caves and passageways inside the hills" that allowed the defenders to move safely to the point of attack.

It was a meatgrinder of a battle and the low point for K Company came in late May 1945 when they relieved another unit on Half Moon Hill. "It was," wrote Gene Sledge, "the most ghastly corner of hell I had ever witnessed. As far as I could see, an area that previously had been a low grassy valley with a picturesque stream meandering through it was a muddy, repulsive, open sore on the land. The place was choked with the putrefaction of death, decay, and destruction... Men struggled and fought and bled in an environment so degrading I believed we had been flung into hell's own cesspool."

Slated to take part in Operation Downfall, the invasion of the Japanese home islands – a campaign that some feared would cost a million American casualties – the surviving Devil Dogs were hugely relieved to hear that the dropping of atomic bombs on Hiroshima and Nagasaki had prompted the Japanese to surrender unconditionally on 15 August 1945.

President Harry S. Truman's decision to drop the bombs still divides opinion today. But the men of K Company were in no doubt that it was the right thing to do. "Some people say," wrote R. V. Burgin, "it was awful us using it. But if they think that was awful, I don't think people have a damn clue what would have happened if we'd hit Japan... We would have killed millions of Japanese, and there's no telling how many of us would have been wounded or killed, going in."

More than 90 members of K Company were killed during the war, and hundreds suffered wounds and psychological trauma. Was their sacrifice worth it? They thought so. "There is no such thing as 'the glory of war'", wrote one. "There is only the 'horror of war' to the men who fight. Unfortunately, until heaven prevails, somebody has got to be ready to defend our country or we'll lose it."

It is a sentiment that resonates today with many Ukrainians – men and women – who are prepared to make the ultimate sacrifice to defend their homeland. Like the Devil Dogs, they are determined not just to fight the enemy to a standstill, but to defeat them and show Putin's government the error of its ways.

Saul David is a bestselling historian and author of *SBS, Silent Warriors: The Authorised Wartime History* and *Devil Dogs: King Company, From Guadalcanal to the Shores of Japan.*

Banged Up Abroad: Ben Macintyre on Colditz

For those prisoners that repeatedly attempted escape, their German captors dispatched them to Colditz Castle, close to Leipzig in Saxony. Here various nationalities competed against each other to escape from this prison of prisons. But there were also other goings on in Colditz, and these have been exposed by Ben Macintyre in his new book, Colditz: Prisoners of the Castle. He met with our editor to discuss a story that up to now was thought to be well-known.

I wanted to talk about the two main themes I got coming out of the book and the first is the reason why the prisoners are all there which is deutschfeindlich. So this is being insufficiently friendly to the Nazis, who are not generally known to be friendly themselves.

But it's fascinating, isn't it? Only the Germans would come up with a word for insufficient friendliness and I'm slightly parodying them there. Yes, Colditz was the place for people who are prisoners, who had either tried to escape from other prison camps or who had made themselves so intolerable that the Germans felt they had to move them all into one place. It turned out to be the spectacularly bad idea because if you put all the bad boys together in one camp, they behave extremely badly and they egg each other on. And that's what gave Colditz, in a way, its very particular atmosphere, was that these were almost hand-picked by the Germans for their recalcitrance, which of course makes for some fascinating characters. I approached this project with some trepidation because Colditz is absolutely buried in our national mythology…but actually the story of Colditz turned out to be very different from [what I expected].

It's partly a story of daring do. It is partly a story of Boys Own, japes and all the games. But actually there's a much darker and much more interesting story to Colditz, it turns out, on digging. There hasn't been a book about Colditz for 20 years and our own perceptions of history have changed radically in the last 20 years. The real story of Colditz, I found, was about class and race and sexuality and a particular kind of madness, because if you lock people up for five years with absolutely no idea whether they're ever going to get out, a particular kind of lunacy sort of takes hold.

And what [the prisoners] did inside Colditz to sort of recreate the world that they'd come from. These were upper middle class, usually public school educated, white men, and they recreated a kind of interwar world inside Colditz, complete with theatrical performances and bridge clubs and societies and exclusivity. It was incredibly socially stratified.

There was even, believe it or not, a Bullingdon Club in Colditz, which was one of the most bizarre discoveries, even inside Colditz, there was a kind of rigid social structure going on.

We can deal with class straight away, because the Bullingdon Club that they set up - and they actually call it the Bullingdon Club, don't they? But there are also a couple of communists there and I was reading it thinking, if there was going to be one thing to turn me over to communism, it would be a Bullingdon Club in a prisoner of war camp.

Yes, they have their own mess and you had to have been a member of the Bullingdon Club. I found that fascinating too, and also slightly contradicting what I've just said. External factors were influencing life inside Colditz. You had, in a way, the battle between the communists and there were people of the extreme right in Colditz, too, believe me, particularly among the French, there were some ferocious antisemites, there were Pétinists, there were people who were sympathetic to the right. And so you have this kind of ideological battle, in a way, taking place inside Colditz that prefigures the Cold War, that prefigures the war itself. So you've got a kind of rolling political debate going at the same time, which is fascinating.

And of course, these are most of them well educated people. They are people used to dealing with ideas. So you've got an intellectual sort of conflict taking place inside the prison walls, as well as this class conflict going on. And there is a conflict among the classes. Something that I had never realised and you'd never have got from the board game, was that although this was an officers prison, this was a place where officers had certain privileges. Under the Geneva Convention, [they] had ordinary soldiers, privates, also prisoners, to work for them.

You mentioned race, and there's one individual there who is an Indian nationalist. He sounds like a fascinating character, but really had a lot of bad luck and was treated terribly, wasn't he?

He was treated very badly. He was the only non-white soldier in Colditz and his story has never been told, I think, I'm afraid, because he doesn't fit into our mythology of Colditz. And he was an extraordinary man: Birendranath Mazumdar. He was the only Indian officer in the Royal Army Medical Corps. He was captured at Dunkirk, taken to Colditz, where, as you rightly say, he suffered appalling racism, but not from the Germans, from the British. He was treated as a second-class citizen, mocked, told he wasn't allowed to escape because his skin was the wrong colour. He'd have been picked up immediately, which might have been true, actually, but it was nonetheless an astonishingly racist thing to insist on. And his story is quite remarkable. I don't want to give it away too much, but it's a story of remarkable heroism, actually. And he gets out. He gets out. I don't want to give it all away about how he did it, but it's one of the many untold stories of Colditz.

Who would have known it after all this time? It's true often, this kind of area of history that the mythology we inherited, the black and white stories, the Sunday afternoon TV, films like The Dam Busters and The Great Escape and so on, they all follow a sort of certain template. That is a story of simple, moral, black and white, goodies and baddies, heroes and villains, and there's not much in between, of course.

I hope what Colditz asks is the question of what would you do? Because the whole of human nature is in there and there are people of astonishing heroism and integrity and ingenuity. And there are others more like me, and others who are sort of somewhere in the middle. They're trying to do the best thing, most of them, and some do the wrong thing. There are traitors, there are Quislings in there. We are all made of human clay. And the idea that somehow everybody in Colditz was a born hero with a bristling moustache is not true.

The prisoners weren't compelled to escape, to attempt to escape were they? One often thinks that the order is to escape.

That was the myth. And in fact, there's a character in The Great Escape who says, "It is every officer's duty to escape." It was not. Nowhere were you required to do this, but many did, and everyone pretty much bar one or two was happy to contribute to the sort of 'escape industry', as it were, to help, to act as [a lookout], to help make disguises and so on. And that is half the fun of Colditz. It's the extraordinary kind of community that built up around how to get out of the damn place. But not everybody was involved in that and you definitely weren't required to.

Indeed, by the end of the time in Colditz, the senior British officer was actively discouraging people from doing it, because by that point, you were likely to end up dead because the whole atmosphere of the war had changed. Hitler had passed the Commando Order. If you were caught out of uniform in Germany, you were quite likely just to be killed. The atmosphere gets darker and it changes over time.

The proportions of foreign officers in the prison. It starts off it's quite multinational, doesn't it, and the French and Dutch have proportionately quite a bit of success?

Yes, it's quite interesting and indeed, they tot up the numbers. It was a kind of 'Escape League'. One of the ways they got through the boredom of the day was to compete with each other. There were alliances, in theory, between the nations, but like alliances, there were also kind of great rivalries. And the Brits - I won't say they were enraged when the French managed to carry out their first escape, but they didn't like it very much. They thought they should be the first ones out, so they all spurred each other on. I found that fascinating, the way that sort of pre-war prejudices about other nations were carried into Colditz. It's an awful lot of national stereotyping going on - all points of the compass around here. Everyone is saying, "the beastly Belgians, all they ever do is lie around eating." It's all completely stereotyped, and the British are lazy and feckless and unreliable in the eyes of the French and so on. All of that is both good fun, but also kind of it's also very instructive, I think, about a certain sort of view of the world that they carried into Colditz with them.

The Poles were very popular, weren't they?

The Poles were much loved because the Poles treated the Germans with absolute disdain, although they themselves were in considerable jeopardy, because, of course, Poland was not a signatory to the Geneva Convention. And from the German point of view, they were very lucky to be in an officer's camp, so they were treated slightly differently. And the Poles were extraordinary. I mean, they were absolutely indefatigable escapers. They also brewed their own kind of booze in the attics of Colditz, which added to their popularity, I think.

There aren't many women in the story, for obvious reasons, but those that are have hugely admirable roles. There's 70-year-old Mrs Walker whose story is extraordinary.

Is extraordinary, isn't it? Isn't it? I mean, again, I went into this thinking it is going to be a book about men, but it's not. And 'Mrs M', as they called her - her Polish name was Markowska…she'd married a Pole, she was from Fife, she was a doughty Scots woman who had, worked for British Intelligence, and she was in charge of the escape routes through Warsaw.

Again, her story has never been told before because she sort of doesn't fit into the kind of narrative that we're used to. When these soldiers got out of Colditz, as you have rightly pointed out, occasionally, but not very often, many of them headed straight for Mrs M because she was the way to get you out of Poland, out of Nazi occupied Poland. She was astonishingly brave and she ran the escape routes and they absolutely adored her. She became a sort of mythological figure inside Colditz. She was already in her sixties or even seventies by the time this is happening, and she would throw these extraordinary secret dinner parties in Warsaw where everyone would toast the King and she would say, "well, we're all going to get out of here."

You can listen to an extended interview with Ben Macintyre on the Aspects of History Podcast when Ben goes on to talk about Kim Philby and the movie based on his book, *Operation Mincemeat*.

Ben Macintyre is writer-at-large for *The Times*, and author of *A Spy Among Friends* and *Colditz: Prisoners of the Castle*, his latest book.

The Origins of Russia's Cult of the Great Patriotic War By Katie Stallard

Fifty years before Vladimir Putin twisted the history of the Second World War to stoke support for his 'special military operation' in Ukraine, the Soviet leadership exploited the memory of the conflict for its own purposes. The New Statesman's Senior Editor on China and Global Affairs looks back at myth-making from previous Russian autocrats.

On a bright spring morning in May 1967, a solitary armoured personnel carrier rumbled through the streets of central Moscow. It was guarded by a phalanx of motorcycle escorts in military uniform, their expressions solemn, eyes fixed firmly ahead, as they formed a protective ring around the dark green hull. Large crowds gathered by the side of the road to watch them pass. In front of the Kremlin, a cluster of men in dark suits stood waiting, arrayed in order of importance around the stocky figure of the new general secretary Leonid Brezhnev.

The armoured car contained the most sacred of cargoes. Inside was a lantern lit from the eternal flame of the revolutionary martyrs' cemetery in Leningrad, where the heroes of the October revolution that brought Lenin to power in 1917 – along with the subsequent civil war – were buried. The symbolic fire had burned in their memory for the last five decades, but now a portion was being transported more than four hundred miles to light a new flame at a new monument in the heart of the capital, that the party leadership hoped would kindle a new source of public support for its rule.

The destination was the new Tomb of the Unknown Soldier commemorating the fallen from the Great Patriotic War, as World War II is known in Russia. The remains of a Soviet soldier had been exhumed from the site of the Battle of Moscow, where the Red Army fought Hitler's troops in the winter of 1941-42, and was re-buried with full military honours at the new memorial in 1966. All that was needed to complete it was to light the new eternal flame.

That the Soviet Union had built a memorial like this was not unusual. Many countries had their own ceremonial arches and cenotaphs. What was strange was that it had taken them so long to do it; that this was all happening two decades after the end of the war, long after the fallen were supposed to have been laid to rest. But this was a reflection of how official attitudes towards the war were shifting. Stalin had cancelled the Victory Day holiday that commemorated the end of the Second World War in Europe in 1947 and claimed the credit for himself. But after his death, Nikita Khrushchev's tenure had allowed a more critical examination of the conflict's history as he denounced Stalin and presided over a cultural 'thaw'. Now Brezhnev was embarking on a new approach as he set about building what would become known as the cult of the Great Patriotic War and rise to the status of a national religion under Vladimir Putin in the following century. This new memorial would function as its central shrine.

The famous fighter pilot and Hero of the Soviet Union Aleksey Maresyev carried the torch with the eternal flame the final few yards and presented it to the waiting Brezhnev, who turned and mounted the steps of the monument alone. He lowered the torch to a gleaming bronze star at its centre, lighting a new flame that has burned there ever since.

It was both a symbolic and an actual passing of the torch as the Communist Party turned to the memory of the conflict to bolster its appeal. In case anyone had missed the symbolism, Moscow party boss Nikolai Yegorychev spelled it out. "This fire," he said, "transfers across an entire half-century the undimmed flame of [the] October [revolution]. ... It is as if the soldiers of the Revolution and the soldiers of the Great Patriotic War have closed ranks into one immortal rank."

The leadership hoped these combined forces would now defend the party's position in power.

By the mid-1960s, the revolution was almost half a century old and the promised socialist utopia no closer to reality. Lenin's portrait and his quotes were all around. But that ubiquity was not the same as genuine enthusiasm. Even as they ordered up new busts and tributes to the former leader, the party was searching for new ideas to cement its popular support. Brezhnev's stolid personality made him a poor candidate for a new charismatic leadership cult. And as future leaders would similarly find, other than the early achievements of the space race, there was little else in recent decades to celebrate.

Lenin had long provided an important source of legitimacy for the party, explained the historian Nina Tumarkin, who researched the cults of Lenin and the Great Patriotic War for her books Lenin Lives! and The Living and the Dead. When Brezhnev took over, there was "really a very full-blown cult" of Lenin, she told me. "I wouldn't say that people were enthusiastic about it, but it was virtually everywhere." The idea was to reinvigorate popular support by combining the memory of the war, which stirred strong emotions, with that of Lenin, which increasingly did not. "The centennial of Lenin's birth was coming up in 1970," Tumarkin said. "So in a sense it was supposed to bring together symbolically the martyrs and the people who had died in the revolution, and by implication perhaps the Red Army during the civil war, with the people who had died in the Great Patriotic War."

Six months after ousting Khrushchev, the new collective leadership headed by Brezhnev reinstated the Victory Day holiday to celebrate the end of the conflict. The twentieth anniversary was approaching on May 9, 1965, and with just over two weeks to go, the ruling Presidium announced that there would be a massive parade through Red Square to mark the occasion. This was not quite as formidable an undertaking as it might sound. Instead of staging a completely new event from a standing start, the plan was to move the traditional parade celebrating Workers' Day on May 1 to May 9 for Victory Day, which was itself an indication of the symbolic shift taking place. They minted new medals for veterans and built a series of new war memorials across the country during the years that followed, which was how the senior ranks of the Communist Party came to be waiting to light their newest eternal flame at the new Tomb of the Unknown Soldier in Moscow on that bright May morning in 1967.

From Magnitogorsk in the Ural Mountains to Murmansk in the Russian arctic, colossal new monuments went up featuring heroic Soviet soldiers in the socialist realist style (which in practice was more propagandistic than realistic), all chiselled hulk and resolute jaws. Many of the new memorials were inscribed with the words of the poet and Leningrad siege survivor Olga Bergholz: "No one is forgotten, nothing is forgotten." This wasn't true. The version of the war the party now wanted to remember involved forgetting plenty.

"Those of us who had fought in the war thought, at first, that at last the war was getting the attention it merited," literary critic Lazar Lazarev, who had served in the Red Army, wrote. "But in fact that attention was purely an official attempt to turn the war into a show made up of concocted legends." Like the towering new monuments with their idealized warriors, the focus was meant to be on the glorious victory and the stories that provided a shining vindication of the Soviet political system, not the suffering and the reality.

In general, the twenty-third Party Congress decided in 1966, there should be 'less gloom' in depictions of the Stalinist past and discussion of the war. In practice, this meant that what scope there had been to research the darker aspects of the war and Stalin's culpability shut down. Where Konstantin Simonov's previous novels, The Living and the Dead and People Are Not Born Soldiers, published in 1959 and 1962, had been praised for their realistic portrayal of the conflict, the third in his trilogy, One Hundred Days of War, was banned by the censors in 1966.

"The truth must be founded on some kind of ideological line," insisted an official from the military archives during a meeting to discuss Simonov's work. Research on the war should focus primarily on heroism and "feats," he said. His comments foreshadowed similar remarks by Putin's Minister of Culture, Vladimir Medinsky, fifty years later, who claimed that protecting the image of Soviet heroism during the war was more important than the truth. "Even if this story were made up from start to finish," Medinsky said in 2016 of a famous tale involving a tank battle on the outskirts of Moscow that turned out to be fabricated. "Even if there had been nothing at all, this is a sacred legend, which simply cannot be touched." Like Brezhnev, Putin would decide that maintaining the glorious myth of the Soviet victory mattered more than the facts.

The Military Publishing House took charge of censoring all memoirs about the war and stripped out all traces of the disastrous early months and Stalin's failure to prepare for the attack. "Not a word could be published about the catastrophic defeats of 1941 or the real reasons they occurred," said Lazar Lazarev. "Nor was a whisper permitted about the astonishing fact that three times as many officers in the Soviet army and navy high commands died in the Stalinist purges of 1937-38 as were killed by Nazi bullets and bombs throughout the war." Even the most celebrated military commanders, he explained, soon found that their memoirs had "as much hope of surviving the savage ministrations of this special commission as a camel of passing through the eye of a needle."

The permitted narrative of the war also excluded the fact that Jewish citizens had been specifically targeted by the Nazis. Rather than focusing on the horrors of the Holocaust that were revealed with the end of the war, Stalin had stoked a new campaign of anti-Semitism and the official Soviet account insisted that Hitler attacked the USSR in general, rather than any one group in particular. As Stanford University historian Amir Weiner recounts in Making Sense of War, when Yad Vashem, the Holocaust archival centre in Jerusalem wrote to the Soviet government in 1965 to request documents on the fate of Soviet Jews, they were told that, the archives "relating to the crimes of German fascism in World War II are not organized according to the nationality of the victims."

Stalin's own role in the conflict was still a sensitive subject. There was no getting around the fact that the war was won under his leadership, but then he had also decimated the senior ranks of the military beforehand, refused to believe that Hitler would attack, and left his troops to suffer heavy losses when he did. There were rumours during the early Brezhnev years that Stalin's corpse would be restored to the Lenin mausoleum in Red Square. This didn't happen, but a large grey stone bust was installed above his grave in the summer of 1970. It was a compromise that reflected his place in this revised version of history. Stalin would not be ignored. His memory would be treated with respect. But there would be no new Stalinist cult. Although this wasn't the end of the story. The late dictator's image would be further rehabilitated in the decades to come after Putin came to power and turned to the war to serve his own political purposes, and to stoke support for his invasion of Ukraine.

Katie Stallard is the author of *Dancing on Bones: History and Power in China, Russia, and North Korea.*

How the Russians See Themselves, by Rodric Braithwaite

With the recent Ukrainian success in the east of the country, the Russian Army is now on the backfoot and it increasingly looks impossible for them to gain any kind of success militarily. With Putin's pronouncements on his nuclear threat, this is consistent with previous rulers' sabre rattling, and speaks to Russia's pride in how it sees itself. Sir Rodric Braithwaite, British Ambassador in Moscow from 1989 to 1992, describes the Russian mindset.

If you want to work out what your opponent is likely to do next, you need to understand how he sees himself.

During the Cold War our judgement of Soviet behaviour was often distorted by prejudice, ignorance, and wishful thinking. Raymond Garthoff, a wise CIA analyst, believed that 'the inability to empathize with the other side and visualize its interests in other than adversarial terms' was one reason why we often got the USSR wrong. We exaggerated the Russians' determination, competence, and power. We failed to realise that they were quite as frightened of us as we were of them. So we were more surprised by the Soviet collapse than we should have been.

We are not doing much better now. Our inability to think our way into the thoughts and emotions of Vladimir Putin and his people means that we are continually, and for the most part unnecessarily, baffled and surprised by what he does.

Each of us has a national narrative, a story we tell ourselves from generation to generation, adapting it to new realities and omitting the bits we find uncomfortable or disgraceful. The British, for example, believe they are the inheritors of a glorious 'Island Story' of undeviating progress from Magna Carta towards power and democracy. They are always surprised to learn that foreigners - especially their former imperial subjects - see them as greedy, brutal, devious and hypocritical.

So too with the Russians. They trace their history back more than a thousand years. The story they tell is profoundly patriotic. It differs greatly from the story told about them by others.

This is what it looks like.

It starts, as most national stories do, with an inadequately documented founding myth. In the eighth or ninth century after Christ, so the legend goes, some Vikings who were called Rus, meaning "men who row", settled at the eastern end of the Baltic Sea. They founded a trading post and later a town on land already inhabited by Finns. Under their leader Ryurik, they raided and traded their way down the great river Dnepr towards the rich empire of Byzantium. On their way they met people called Slavs. The two combined. The Vikings adopted the language of the Slavs. The Slavs, a disorganised lot, welcomed the superior organising skills of the Varangians.

Together they set up a great city called Kiev - or Kyiv in Ukrainian. In the ninth century their Grand Prince Vladimir, a descendant of Ryurik, adopted the Orthodox Christianity practiced in Byzantium. Kievan Rus became one of the most sophisticated states in Christendom, a conglomerate of princedoms ruled by the Ryurik dynasty and stretching from the Baltic to the Black Sea. Its inhabitants thought the Catholics to their west were heretical and hostile. They still do.

In 1242 disaster struck when the Mongols utterly destroyed Kiev and the princedoms in the South. But those in the North survived, still under Ryurik rule. At first they paid the Mongols tribute, then they wriggled free. Dmitri Donskoi defeated the Mongols in battle. Ivan III "the Great" of Moscow successfully bought the so-called "Mongol Yoke" to an end.

Ivan the Great set out to reassemble the ancient lands of Kievan Rus. He centralised the northern princedoms into a state which people called "Muscovy". He began to recover those bits of Kievan Rus into which Poles, Lithuanians, Turks, and Crimean Tartars had moved as the Mongols withdrew.

It was a protracted process, completed by Catherine the Great. She defeated the Turks to obtain Ukraine and Crimea. She joined with the Prussians and the Austrians to partition Poland and erase it from the map. She saw no need for excuses: the territories "belonged in antiquity to Russia, where the cities were built by Russian princes and the population descends from the same tribe as the Russians and are also of our same [Orthodox] faith." She struck a medal which read: "I have recovered what was torn away." Putin uses the same language when he talks about Ukraine.

Many Russians praise Ivan III and his autocratic successors because they believe Russia is too large to be except by a strong hand. Once again, Catherine summed it up: *"The Sovereign is absolute; for there is no other Authority but that which centres in his single person, that can act with a Vigour proportionate to the extent of such a vast Dominion"*. A recent Russian blogger put it like this: "Ivan the Terrible, like Joseph Stalin, is one of the most slandered Russian rulers. and you can understand why. They built a strong Russia and harshly suppressed Western attempts to establish political, economic, or ideological control over it. Under Ivan the Terrible Russia became an empire. ... [The autocracy] has existed for four centuries and guarantees Russia's power, which is why the West dislikes it."

Byzantium fell to the Turks in 1453, leaving Russia as the chief champion of Orthodoxy against Rome and its heresies. Many Russians believe that Peter the Great's drive to Westernise his country was a dangerous distraction from Dostoevsky [who] was not the first nor the last to believe that Russia's overriding mission was to bring Truth to a corrupted, worldly, and heretical Europe. The Soviets shared this sense of Russia's mission: but for them it was Communism, not Orthodoxy. The Russian Orthodox Patriarch, and Vladimir Putin, still proclaim the moral superiority of today's Orthodox Russia.

Putin is far from the first Russian to believe that an envious West has always been unremittingly hostile to Russia and determined to destroy it. After all, their country has been invaded time out of mind. In the early centuries the invaders were nomads, Mongols, Poles, Lithuanians, Germans, Danes, and Swedes. In the seventeenth century the Poles captured Moscow and practically extinguished the Russian state. Napoleon nearly did the same in 1812. The British invaded Russia in the nineteenth and twentieth centuries. Americans, Japanese, and French, soldiers joined them in an unsuccessful attempt to strangle the Bolshevik revolution.

Then the perfidious British and French tried to turn Hitler's aggression eastwards. They were cunningly outmanoeuvred by Stalin, who built his defences by occupying Poland and the Baltic States in agreement: an entirely legitimate defensive manoeuvre. When Hitler nevertheless treacherously attacked the Soviet Union in June 1941, the Russians roundly defeated him. It cost them 27 million dead. Many believe that the Soviet Union won thanks above all to Stalin's far-sighted if brutal construction of a massive defence industry before the war, and his inspired leadership during it. Russians who reject Stalin and all his works remain passionately proud of that victory.

The West never showed its gratitude for having been saved from Hitler by the Soviet Union. Instead it did their best to undermine the alliance which the Soviet Union had constructed with the countries of Eastern Europe as a barrier against further aggression. America attempted to use its monopoly of the nuclear weapon to blackmail its former ally. Thus, the West launched the Cold War. The Russians had no choice but to match them.

In 1991 Western subversion and domestic treachery nevertheless brought a great nation to its knees. The Soviet Union fell apart. Large parts were torn away to become independent. The loss of Ukraine was especially painful: it had after all been an integral part of Russia since the days of Kievan Rus. NATO, the most powerful and threatening alliance in history, expanded despite the promises of Western politicians. The West used its drunken puppet Boris Yeltsin to peddle ideas about "democracy" and "human rights" deliberately intended to undermine the essence of what it meant to be Russian.

For many Russians all this was an unbearable humiliation. Vladimir Putin restored their country to prosperity, order, and international respect. He rooted out the traitors and the corrupt. His methods were traditionally severe, but that was a reasonable price to pay. Russians were even prepared to support him in war, if that was what it took to frustrate

Western intrigues in Ukraine, and restore it to its rightful place as part of Russia's ancient lands.

This self-serving view of Russian history conceals an underlying lack of confidence. Though they are convinced of their spiritual superiority, Russians have always been uneasily aware that they could not match the West's technological sophistication. Ivan III was only the first Russian ruler to find himself importing Western weapons. If Russia is so self-evidently superior to the West, why do its repeated attempts to catch up so regularly fail? The knowledgeable and perceptive American scholar-diplomat George Kennan spoke of the latent suspicion in every Russian soul that "the hand of failure lies heavily over all Russian undertaking, that the term "Russia" does not really signify a national society destined to know power and majesty, but only a vast unconquerable expanse of misery, poverty, inefficiency, and mud."

It is an intriguing counterpoint to the defiant rhetoric.

The story naturally looks completely different to Russia's immediate neighbours. For them the Russians were predatory barbarians, Asiatics, not European at all. The father of the Anglo-Polish writer, Joseph Conrad, was imprisoned and exiled by the Russians. He wrote *"We Poles have suffered slaughter, conflagration, robbery, rape and torture in the hands of Muscovy, The whole of Muscovy is a prison [...] corrupted and infested with vermin."* Poles remember that their Polish-Lithuanian Commonwealth was once the most powerful state in Eastern Europe until it was wiped out by Catherine and her Prussian and Austrian colleagues. The Polish state was reborn in 1918, only to be wiped out again in 1939 by Hitler and Stalin, and restored in 1945 only as a Soviet satellite.

Passions run high among Ukrainians too, but for them the story is more complicated. One Ukrainian historian recently described the Russians as the direct inheritors of the Mongols, *"horrible in their lack of education, rage and cruelty. These people had no use for European culture and literacy. All such things like morality, honesty, shame, justice, human dignity and historical awareness were absolutely foreign to them"*. Many Ukrainians would agree, and insist that modern Russia, which emerged as "Muscovy" from the Mongol Yoke, has no connection with Kievan Rus.

But many other Ukrainians are ambiguous. They are bound to Russia by family and linguistic ties. They do not want to have to choose between Russia and the West, but would prefer to have decent relations with both. Putin has gone far to change their minds.

When Putin told President George W Bush in 2008 that "Ukraine is not even a state", he was of course talking nonsense. Europe is full of states which did not exist a century earlier, and the clock cannot be put back.

But his version of history is not entirely inaccurate: if it were, it would be impossible to sustain. As with all such national stories, the facts are jumbled together with the myths and the fantasies, and the awkward and disgraceful bits are left out. But it hardly matters whether it is "true" in any sense that would be recognised by a professional historian. People are driven by their emotions and their beliefs rather than by what other people may regard as the facts. So it is with Putin's Russians.

And national stories can change under the pressure of events. The Germans and the Japanese reinvented themselves as peace-loving nations after they were totally defeated in 1945. The great European empires crumbled away after the war, regardless of the hopes and wishes of those who had ruled them. It makes little sense to try to predict Russia's future at this bleak moment. But by the same token one should not rule out the possibility that it will one day learn to live in peace and prosperity with its neighbours.

Sir Rodric Braithwaite is a diplomat and writer, and author of *Russia: Myths and Realities*.

A Close Run Thing: Max Hastings on the Cuban Missile Crisis

In the autumn of 1962, the Soviet Union and the United States faced off in the Caribbean Sea over the matter of nuclear weapons on the island of Cuba. Placed there in a supreme act of recklessness by Khrushchev, for thirteen days the world held its breath as the two sides pushed each other to the brink of annihilation. Max Hastings has written a new book on the crisis, and he met our editor to discuss the events and personalities.

Max, it's an opportune moment to talk about your new book Abyss, since we're now at another showdown with nuclear conflict being threatened. Of course, it's the 60th anniversary of the Cuban Missile Crisis, yet here we are again…

Well, when I started out on this book, it felt like writing another piece of history and it was an odd one out among my works because all the past ones have been about wars that happened. This one, of course, was about a war that, mercifully for mankind, didn't actually happen, but came so close. So many people, it has to be said, on both sides of the Iron Curtain, as we called it, in the middle of the Cold War, actually wanted it to happen. They wanted war. It is a sort of miracle that it didn't happen. But when I started out it just felt like this was all to do with the past. But now, suddenly again, we see in the Kremlin another reckless risk-taker who is prepared repeatedly to expose the west to nuclear threats and who, I believe, to be a less responsible player than was Nikita Khrushchev, the Soviet Union's leader in 1962. So suddenly the whole thing has an importance to try and understand what happened 60 years ago and what lessons we can learn for the future. And of course, the first lesson for everybody is: be afraid! We've all had such spoilt existences in the last 30, 40 years. It may not have seemed so, but when you look at it, we haven't been involved in big wars, only small wars, a long way away. But it's only in recent years that climate change has suddenly started to be a big factor. Nobody has been obliged to fight. We've had enough to eat, we've been warm, we've been comfortable. Therefore, we've been able to set aside in our minds the huge risk that these nuclear weapons, which terrified the world in all the years of the Cold War, have always been there. And now suddenly dangerous tyrants are rattling them all over again and we begin to see how the world felt in 1962.

The current chiefs of defence staff in America nowadays seem to be a lot more aware of the horrific consequences of nuclear war. And so there doesn't appear to be as much 'missile rattling' as you describe it.

I'd entirely agree with you that as far as we know, thank goodness, there's no counterpart of Curtis LeMay among the American chiefs of staff. But in those days, one has to remember that all these people had grown up in the Second World War. Many of them had fulfilled senior roles. Curtis LeMay made his reputation by incinerating half of Japan by leading the bomber operations that killed hundreds of thousands. He came home at the end of the war to be hailed as a national hero. Also in 1945, the United States had led the Western world to an absolute victory. The idea of absolute victory was still very deeply instilled in people's heads. The leaders of America had no doubt at all that they were the leader of by far the most powerful and important state on the planet. And they wanted to see America use its power to secure its end, to secure absolute victory.

Today there's an understanding that absolute victories are not on the table, and people are much more cautious. They realise it would almost certainly be the end of the planet if we go to nuclear war. In 1962 a scary number of people did not understand that. It is pretty spooky when you look back to those days.

With President Kennedy it certainly is his finest hour. And Robert Kennedy as well, his closest adviser, seems to have had a conversion. He was a very bombastic, confrontational individual, but he also takes the same line as his brother during the crisis.

Bobby, I think was pretty unlovable character, whereas there's not much doubt that, especially in his handling of the Western leadership in the Cold War, Kennedy displayed greatness. His brother, in my eyes, was never more than a charismatic politician, even on a good day. But in the missile crisis, he did display extraordinary common sense, and while some of his first reactions weren't very smart, he realised almost as soon as his brother that invading Cuba was a last resort and not the first one. He backed his brother all the way. When his brother said, "we're going to have a blockade," which the chiefs of staff called a pathetic response, Bobby realised that you've got to try every other expedient diplomatic and minimal force, which is what the blockade represented before you went to shooting. And in that sense, Bobby came out of the crisis remarkably well.

Now, on the plans for the invasion of Cuba. You've just mentioned that LeMay came out of World War II with this great reputation. Maxwell Taylor, who may be familiar to some from Operation Market Garden, reading your book, I was almost open mouthed at how they seem to make so many assumptions and it didn't seem to be really well thought out at all.

The intelligence was lousy. The CIA thought that the Russians had about 5,000 troops on Cuba instead of 43,000. They really did. They had no inkling about the tactical nuclear weapons and it was only very late in the crisis that some of the people around the table in the White House began to understand that the invasion of Cuba was going to be a very bloody business, not just for the Russians and the Cubans, but also for the American forces doing the invading. But there was this huge residual arrogance in the United States. One of the things

I've tried to do in my book (a lot of the books about the crisis just deal with the 13 days) is to set it in the wider context of the Cold War. So that anybody who reads the book will first of all understand something about what Cuba was in those days, and Castro, quite a bit about what the Soviet Union was and Nikita Khrushchev. And quite a lot about what sort of country the United States was in those days. With this curious combination. This curious ambivalence in the United States.

On the one hand, there was this extraordinary national confidence that here was the United States enjoying a stupendous economic success, a standard of living undreamt of 10 or 15 years earlier. And this came with a huge belief that the US really did seem to have been chosen by God, and God was still very important to them, to lead the world and be the most important and richest country on earth. But matched with this was paranoia about the communist threat, a belief that out there were these evil communists who wanted to take it all away from them. So it was a curious mixture of conceit and paranoia.

I also think, and to me this is very important, the quality of the debates in the upper reaches if you leave the mad US military out of it. God, they were clever people around the White House table. One is so impressed by the sort of stuff that was said and the tone of the discussions. And one does worry that nowadays, whether in Britain or America or whatever, you wonder if the same quality of leadership is there.

Jack Kennedy, I'm afraid I'm not a hero worshipper, but I'm just aware by how brilliantly Kennedy conducted himself. I mean, apart from anything else, how anybody could make jokes in those extraordinary circumstances. One day he looked around the table in the cabinet room and he said, "this is the day when we're all going to earn our pay and you better hope that your solution isn't the one that's adopted." Well, this sort of gallows humour, it does increase one's respect for Kennedy, that anybody could make jokes in those circumstances.

The Joint Chiefs didn't seem to have much respect for Kennedy. When LeMay says to Kennedy, "You're in one hell of a spot" or something similar.

Amazingly, the sheer the insults that LeMay at the White House table heaped on Kennedy, he said, "You're in one hell of a fix." And Kennedy, The President of the United States, looks at him and he said, "what do you mean?" LeMay doubled [down] and he said, "you are in one hell of a fix." Kennedy kept his temper, but he said, "and you are right there in it with me personally."

Everybody else around the table obviously was stunned that this mad Air Force general had the nerve to talk to the President of the United States in this way. What was more incredible was that LeMay kept his job until his formal retirement two years down the track, after Lyndon Johnson had succeeded Kennedy. And it's amazing, but of course, he was a very famous man, Curtis LeMay. He made this terrific reputation and Kennedy didn't dare to sack him. Now, I'm not surprised you [don't] sack him in the middle of the missile crisis…but one is amazed that when it was all over, he didn't…Kennedy said after the crisis, "the military are mad", and so they were.

It was amusing to see the LeMay then ends up as Vice Presidential candidate, along with George Wallace, the racist Governor of Alabama in the 1968 campaign.

Oh, yeah. He was a right-wing lunatic and he was straight out of Doctor Strangelove. Actually a lot of the stuff one read, because I read an enormous number of transcripts of oral history interviews with senior Air Force generals after the crisis was over, and instead of saying, "phew, thank goodness our President got us out of this," most of them were still after the crisis saying, "the President let us down. They were just wimps. We could have had a great victory."

"We could have cleaned out that rat's nest," as one Air Force general said, of Cuba, "and we could have got rid of Castro, we could have got rid of all the communists in Latin America." And they were saying this after the crisis. They weren't saying, "thank God we've averted nuclear war."

There's a very good quote you give right at the beginning, which is probably a good way to end our chat. Kennedy says to J.K.Galbraith, "You will never know how much bad advice I received."

That's absolutely true.

Sir Max Hastings is the bestselling and acclaimed historian and author of *Vietnam: An Epic Tragedy, 1945-1975*. *Abyss: The Cuban Missile Crisis 1962* is his latest book. You can listen to a full interview with Max on the Aspects of History Podcast.

The AoH Book Club: Giles Milton on Paradise Lost: Smyrna, 1922

The destruction of Smyrna in 1922, for which we've just seen the centenary, was an event that not only shamed the Turkish forces that carried it out, but also the allied navies that looked on as tens of thousands of innocent men, women and children were killed, and hundreds of thousands forced to flee their homes. Giles Milton has written a compelling account of the humanitarian disaster, one of the most tragic of the 20th century, and one that remains unknown.

Giles, Paradise Lost is a riveting account of the events in September 1922 when the now Turkish city of Izmir, then Smyrna, was partially destroyed when Turkish forces entered the city. It is described on the front cover as 'Islam's city of tolerance'. What was Smyrna like prior to the events of September 1922?

In the early 20th century, Smyrna was an extraordinarily cosmopolitan, multi-ethnic, and tolerant city – so much so, that the American expatriate community named their district of the city 'Paradise' (hence the title of my book). They knew of nowhere in America that displayed such an open-minded spirit.

Smyrna was also unique in being the only major city in the Middle East with a majority Christian population.

It was divided into quarters, with specific populations living in each quarter. The city was dominated by the Greeks, who numbered 320,000 and had a virtual monopoly on the lucrative trade in figs, sultanas, and apricots. Greeks also owned many of the city's major businesses.

The second largest population was the Turks, who numbered 140,000; they were mostly artisans and craftsmen who lived in the city's poorest quarter. Despite their humble status, Smyrna's governor was always Turkish, as befitted one of the principal cities in Ottoman Turkey.

Smyrna was also home to a vibrant and wealthy Armenian community, and a smaller Jewish population. There were also European merchants, often insurance brokers and bankers, whose prosperous businesses were centred on Frank Street, the city's principal artery.

The American quarter, Paradise, was smaller but nevertheless important, for it was home to influential educational and humanitarian institutions. Americans also owned the highly profitable Standard Oil Company.

Lastly, there were the Levantines, the wealthiest and most fascinating community in Smyrna. They were descendants of European merchants who had married into the Greek and Armenian communities. Rich, powerful and polyglot, they spoke five or six languages and owned the city's most successful international businesses. The grandest Levantine dynasties lived in palatial villas in the suburb of Bournabat, where they would host splendid cocktail parties in their private botanical gardens.

Why did you want to write the story of this huge event in 20th century European history?

Smyrna in the early years of the twentieth century was like a mirror of our contemporary cities - a melting pot of nationalities and religions. I was interested to learn how a city that functioned so smoothly could be so dramatically torn apart. It begged an important question: could our own contemporary cities suffer a similar fate?

The destruction of Smyrna is also crucial to our understanding of the 20th century world, yet it remains almost a wholly unknown chapter of history. Who knows about the Greek invasion of Turkey in 1919? About the mass exchange of populations in 1923? These were events that transformed the lives of millions of people – almost always for the worse.

Yet more tantalising was the invidious role played by the great powers, notably Britain and America, who were to display a callous disregard for the lives of the refugees trapped on the quayside of Smyrna, even though they had done so much to inflame the situation.

Why were Greece and Turkey at war?

In the aftermath of the Great War, Greece's Prime Minster was a brilliant individual named Eleftherios Venizelos. His central thesis – his Megali Idea –was to reclaim all the ancient Greek lands of Asia Minor, lands that currently fell within the frontiers of the crumbling Ottoman empire. Deploying charm and guile, he persuaded the Great Powers to allow him to occupy Smyrna, with its majority Greek population, in 1919.

When the Turks fought back, Venizelos was obliged to push his troops into the hinterland around Smyrna. But they still came under attack, requiring him to push them even further east. Over the next three years, the Greek army drove ever deeper into Anatolia as it sought to create a safe buffer zone around Smyrna.

The Greek army was victorious for as long as the Great Powers provided it with weapons. But when Venizelos lost power, and the detested King Constantine returned to the Greek throne, the flow of arms ceased. The Turkish nationalists seized their opportunity, crushing the Greek army and advancing towards Smyrna.

There was a western military presence at the port, in the form of 21 British, American and French ships. Why did they not intervene?

The destruction of Smyrna could have been prevented by the Allied warships in the bay of Smyrna. The Great Powers could also have prevented the massacre that followed. But the commanders of those Western warships were under strict orders not to intervene in the unfolding crisis.

Why? Because politicians in London and Washington knew that the Turkish Nationalists had won the war against the Greeks and they were already eyeing up the rich trade deals they were hoping to conclude with Mustafa Kemal (later Ataturk). They didn't want to be seen to be helping tens of thousands of defeated Greeks and Armenians trapped on the quayside.

There is some dispute over who was responsible for the burning of Smyrna, and debate has raged in the 100 years since – where does that responsibility lie in your view?

The great fire of Smyrna remains a controversial subject. Even today, Greeks and Turks violently disagree on who set fire to the city.

I had an open mind when researching the book. I was particularly interest in the eyewitness accounts of the Levantines and Americans because these communities were rarely partisan. They simply recorded the facts.

I unearthed scores of their testimonies – recorded in diaries, letters and memoirs – which left me in no doubt that Turkish soldiers willingly and deliberately set fire to the city. One of the most powerful accounts was by Miss Minnie Mills, head of the American Collegiate Institute. She watched Turkish soldiers dousing Armenian houses in petrol and then setting fire to them.

It is notable that the fire started on a day when the wind had changed direction. This meant that the Greek, Armenian and European districts of the city were in grave danger of being engulfed in flames, whereas the Turkish quarter was likely to remain untouched. This was indeed what happened.

The book was published in Turkey, which in itself is remarkable given your criticism of Turkish forces. What was the reaction there?

My Turkish publisher was an enlightened individual. He told me he thought it was important for the book to be published in Turkish, even though he did not agree with my conclusions. He even got me an invitation to the Istanbul book fair.

The book has received a great deal of criticism in the Turkish press and on the Turkish internet. I was warned not to read some of the more offensive and threatening comments.

One man, Asa Jennings, carried out an incredible act of heroism. How did he manage to save 350,000 people?

There are occasions when history throws up the most unlikely heroes. Asa Jennings is one such individual. An American missionary in Smyrna, Jennings worked for the local branch of the YMCA. Shy, and slight of stature, he had achieved little of note in his adult life. He might easily have fled Smyrna when Turkish troops began destroying the city, for American nationals were being evacuated to the US warships anchored in the bay. But Jennings was appalled by the brutal scenes taking place on the quay of Smyrna and decided to act – in spectacular fashion.

Acting with uncustomary bravado, he pretended to be a high-ranking American official in command of the (non-existent) Western rescue mission. In this guise, he contacted the Greek government in Athens and ordered them to give him immediate command of the 25 Greek vessels standing idle off the coast of Smyrna. To his astonishment, the Greek ministers agreed.

Over the days that followed, Jennings oversaw the rescue of hundreds of thousands of refugees. They were plucked from the quayside of Smyrna and taken to safety on nearby Mytilene island. It was to prove one of the greatest rescue missions of the early 20th century.

If you were to write a new edition, is there anything you'd change?

Yes. A couple of years after publication, I stumbled across a highly detailed account of the Smyrna inferno written by Miss Minnie Mills, whose shorter testimony had already proved invaluable. Eight pages long, this unique account covers events from 5 to 13th September.

I found it in the archives of the American College of Greece where it had lain – forgotten - for more than eight decades. It begins: 'I saw a Turk officer in uniform coming out of a house, taking with him tin containers full of petrol…' Miss Mills was in no doubt that the Turkish army deliberately torched the city.

We are at the 100-year anniversary. Given the mass population shifts in the wake of the disaster, do feelings remain raw in Greece and Turkey?

The destruction of Smyrna remains an extremely sensitive subject in both Greece and Turkey. I was recently asked to participate in a Greek TV documentary about the events of 1922. Our TV crew was one of many Greek teams attempting to make a programme focussed on the anniversary.

All of these teams – with the exception of ours – were refused permission to film in Turkey. Erdogan's government is committed to ensuring that the anniversary commemorations will be as subdued as possible.

Giles Milton is an acclaimed and bestselling historian and author of *Checkmate in Berlin, Nathaniel's Nutmeg* and *Churchill's Ministry of Ungentlemanly Warfare. Paradise Lost* was published in 2008 and is highly recommended. You can listen to two interviews with Giles on the Aspects of History Podcast, on Berlin after the war, and on Smyrna.

Short Story: The Prisoner, by MJ Porter

Normandy, 1064

I'm the last of my family, and as I sit here, bounded by four unyielding walls, it grows daily less and less likely that I'll ever continue my family line. We, who rose from little, and achieved so much, will die out here, in a prison of my king's making.

I know that I'm to blame. I must lack the skills of reconciliation and compromise that my sister, my brother, father, grandfather and even great-grandfather possessed. If those attributes had been mine, then I'd not be here now.

Or so I torture myself—a life of solitude with my thoughts. There's no need for knives and blades to injure, for the threat of a cruel death to kill me, for fear of the unknown to drive me insane. I can do just fine on my own, locked up away from the sights and smells of what it means to be a man, from the touch of another person, with only myself to talk to and against whom to argue.

However, I know I'm too harsh on myself. My family has done what no other has done, well apart from the destroyed royal House of Wessex, direct descendants from the ancient Cerdic, first of his name, half a millennia ago, or so they would have everyone believe. But the House of Wessex had many twists and turns to it, and most would laugh at the outrageous claim now. The House of Wessex was as rotten as any other. In the end.

The House of Leofwine had held its position longer than any other family. Ever. Even those descended from kings. It was inevitable that our luck and skill would run out eventually.

We've survived the reigns of seven capricious Kings of England, with the eighth proving too much for us. Not that he's a real King of England. But I digress.

We've endured war and factionalism, the demands of petty men, the blades of mighty warriors, and some not so mighty, the greed of power-mad kings, the rantings of women who would have destroyed us all, the threat of Viking Raiders kings who tried to eradicate us before we'd even begun. Through it all, we've prospered. Until now, and the new world 'order' that's taken hold of England and all but destroyed her in the last twenty years. Twenty years in which I've been captive to the whim of a man who succeeded when he shouldn't – a man surprised, and terrified, of all that he achieved with hardly any effort.

I hear, even in my prison, the soft scamper of a whisper, the heavy tread of a command, the salt of the bereaved. I know much more than a man blind to the outside world should know, and none of it is good.

He came as a Norman, a Duke, and a man of honour, but he's the worst of all of his ancestors, the Viking Raiders. The very worst.

He came as a Norman, in the dress of a mighty and Godly warrior, enshrined in the golden light of a false Heaven, with swords and arrows as his angels, but he held the morals and greed of a monster, the devil himself.

He's not English. He never will be. He's a Norman. A bastard Norman, at that, though none like to say it too loudly for fear of being overheard and punished.

Even now, it's taken me nearly twenty long and lonely years to realise that all optimism is gone. I'll never take my place as rightful earl of Mercia. I'll never walk the paths my forebears were proud to call home.

Those mausoleums of my family's strength will at no time hold my dead body or be honoured by my presence. I can only grieve here for all those I've lost: for those who I never knew but to whom I owed my position of strength and power; all those I've failed.

Yet, if my family's past has taught me anything, it is that I should never give up. Fate is not inevitable, as those who taunt me within these four walls would have me believe. I do not know what waits around the corner and who the Lord will call to his heavenly side next, upsetting the current political balance. I do not know, and every unknown is a possibility to be exploited when it comes along. So I try to hone my mind, to stay sharp, to banish the monotony of my prison and the futility of my crushed hopes.

I sit, and I wait, or I pace, and I rail, or I sob, and I shudder in my tiny prison. I replay my family's past through my mind to see if I should have acted differently and gained when I lost or where a hard-won gain led to an eventual loss. And sometimes, I fear I can hear my brother and sister, father, my grandfather and great-grandfather talking inside my head, offering me their sage words of advice, assuring me that I did my best and that they would have done the same.

Or, as sometimes happens, they argue and shout, angry words exchanged in the vacuum of my head, and I listen, and I learn, for without belief there is nothing, and if belief is all I have, then I have no intention of giving it up. Ever. No matter the tedium of my circular thoughts.

I'm a prisoner not because of who I am but because of what I am – a reminder of the past and an unwelcome one at that. And all men who fear the past have good reason to, and King William, as he is known, is only too aware of his failures and his greed; of the lies he has built his life upon; of the luck that has made him king of England when he was nothing but a duke and a feeble one at that.

I do not fear my past; neither do I long for it. I would change nothing other than the outcome of my lost battles. I fought for my future, for my England, and I can forever be proud of that, even here, in my exiled imprisonment, with no one but myself for company.

I did not fear to stand my ground, to hold faithful to the oaths given by my brother, father and grandfather to the people of England, to the Kings of England and the Viking Raiders of Denmark and Norway, even occasionally Sweden.

I did not quake before the invader, the spawn of all the worst that the Viking Northerners had to offer. No, I battled him, and them, determined to drive yet another aside, even when he came festooned in the regalia of a righteous man, with the banners of Christ proclaiming his entitlement.

England belongs to the English, no matter what the Normandy Duke might think, and one day he will die, and the illusion of his power will shatter, just as it always does when a king leaves his throne unguarded. No matter how powerful, feared, and tyrannical, no man can ever leave a kingdom to the next generation unchanged. Cracks will always appear, shining a light on the unjust regime of a man grown fat on the proceeds of a lie, and those cracks are there to be exploited, as they must be.

Yet, even I can admit that twenty years is too long for one man to stand alone, especially one as reviled as he is, and one as cruel – always cruel, as those salted sighs inform me, time and time again, hammering against my prison, reminding me that not only am I trapped, I'm also useless to combat the menace of this Normandy Duke.

***

And then I have my wish.

The crack of a door, the shuffle of whispers on wooden floors, the spilling of light into a room too long-shuttered and bolted against the outside world. And into it strides a man I've never known; a warrior in shimmering iron and fire, a hand steady on his sword at his hip, an odd fashion, I notice with some annoyance, as I'm blinking, eyes weeping at the strange twist of fate that has brought me to this.

I'm an old man, or rather, an older man, a shrivelled wreck, dried from my time indoors, hollowed by my seemingly desperate need to escape, to restore myself to all that I once had. I know, if only I could win free, that men and women would flock to my banner, the twin-headed eagle of the House of Leofwine, the righteous banner of a family too long denied their place in England's governance.

"The King is dead," clangs like a bell through my silent mind, splintering the essence of my futility.

"Long live the King," is further intoned, and I know and understand, that just as I thought, all men must die, and all men must be replaced by another, perhaps in their image, but somehow 'lesser,' always 'lesser.' No man, or woman, has yet managed to outlive the time allotted to them.

A strange sensation over tight lips, hot, bursting, perhaps even painful, as my hand tugs on my face, feeling upturned skin, cheeks tight with delight. And music bubbles from my mouth and erupts into the sterile cavern of my imprisonment.

The iron giant stands before me, an expressionless saviour.

"You've been given your freedom."

The words drop like arrows into my feverish mind, each one piercing more deeply than the other until they reach the shadow of the man I used to be; an earl in my own name, the brother of the king's wife, the brother of an earl, the son of an earl, the grandson of an earl, the great-grandson of an ealdorman.

The giant leaves me, and I hear the clamour of his passage as I stand, first a little taller, and then a little straighter, and then far taller, far straighter, the weight of who I was tensing my soul and my body, returning me to who I was when I was locked up twenty years ago.

My laughter dries to a resounding silence.

The door to my prison is open, just hanging there, the wood, bared against my passage for so many years, gleaming enticingly. The light of the bright day on the pitted surface shows me where I've hammered against its solidity, demanded it yields to my entreaties, always in vain, only the indentations of my knuckles a testament to my actions. All that I've accomplished in twenty years.

Now it awaits me and my first steps to freedom, to a life I should have had.

A final glance around my prison shows me how little I've become. There is nothing for me here. Not now, and never again.

I take a step toward freedom, my boots old and creased, just as I am. But then I pause and swallow.

This has been my dream—all these years: to walk, unwatched from the confines of my exile.

I swallow again, my throat dry against the promise of freedom and a future so long denied me.

But, I'm an earl, the brother of an earl, the son of an earl, the grandson of an earl and the great-grandson of an ealdorman. I know who I am and what I am.

Without a backward glance, I stride through that door and into my future.

It's been too long in coming.

M.J.Porter is a bestselling novelist and author of *The Son of Mercia*.

Winters in the World, by Eleanor Parker

The Anglo-Saxon period was rich in culture, with festivals, customs and traditions linked to only two seasons. As Christianity took hold, those blended into a new calendar. Eleanor Parker takes us into this world that is both alien and familiar, though very much lost.

'A person cannot become wise before he has had his share of winters in the world', wrote an Anglo-Saxon poet, just over a thousand winters ago. By this he meant that your 'winters in the world', which make you wise, are the years of your life; this is a poetic way of reckoning a person's age, and suggesting that time brings wisdom. In the minds of early medieval poets, though, winter implied much more than that. It's the season of long nights and hostile weather, when the cold gets into your bones and the spirit is frozen into numbness, unable to do anything more than wait and endure until the spring comes again. Winter is a potent image for a season of trial, and so for this poet the 'share of winters' we live through is our individual portion of this world's suffering, in which no one can escape having a share.

In some ways, the cycle of seasons known to Anglo-Saxon poets like this was one with which we're still intimately familiar. The turning of the year from winter to summer, through the green shoots of spring and the tawny leaves of autumn, is something we all experience every year of our lives. But our ways of thinking about the seasons, and the associations that we have with them, can be very different from how people in the past have experienced that cycle. The experience of the year as charted in Anglo-Saxon life and literature involved a combination of various factors: the changing patterns of light and darkness, cold and warmth, which enabled different ways of living and fostered different states of mind; the rhythms of agriculture and tasks of daily work that varied with the seasons; and the traditional customs and religious festivals that marked stages in the passing of the year.

It was the last of these which changed most radically over the six centuries of the Anglo-Saxon period, and which makes this such a significant and formative stage in the history of the English festival year. In the sixth century, the peoples of Anglo-Saxon England were predominantly pagan; they had their own religious calendar, their own festivals, and their own ways of thinking about the cycle of the year. Formed in a northern European world, that calendar was markedly different from anything we would recognise today. According to Bede, the eighth-century Northumbrian monk who is almost our only written source for the pagan Anglo-Saxon calendar, their year had only two seasons, summer and winter, rather than the four-season model we're familiar with. The two solstices, Midsummer and Midwinter, were the key turning-points of the year, and the year began at the winter solstice, with a mysterious festival called *Modraniht*, 'mothers' night' - perhaps a celebration of mother goddesses. They had their own calendar of months, some named after stages in the agricultural cycle, such as *Þrymilce* (May), the month when cattle could be milked three times a day, or *Weodmonað* (August), 'the month of weeds'; other months, Bede says, got their names from pagan deities, such as *Hreðmonað* (March) and *Eastermonað* (April), named for the goddesses Hreða and Eostre.

But even at the time Bede was writing in the 720s, these names were falling out of use and this seasonal model was in the process of being replaced by something very different. Over the course of the seventh century the kingdoms of Anglo-Saxon England converted to Christianity, and with the new religion came an entirely new calendar. It was a calendar which had grown up in a cultural world far from northern Europe, developing over the course of the first centuries of the Christian church with significant influence from Jewish and Roman calendars. This calendar brought new ways of calculating time, based on the Julian calendar, which first introduced to England the Latin-derived month-names we use today; Hreðmonað and Weodmonað became March and August, named for Roman gods and emperors rather than the goddesses of the Anglo-Saxons.

The Christian calendar also brought a cycle of new festivals: Christmas and Easter, Candlemas and Whitsun, Michaelmas, Martinmas and many more. All these festivals first came to England in the Anglo-Saxon period, and the names by which they're known today go back to Old English roots. In celebrating these feasts, the Anglo-Saxons joined the customs of the wider international church, but they generally gave their own English names to these festivals, sometimes borrowing names from the pre-conversion calendar - as with Easter, taken from the old *Eastermonað*. The core elements of the Christian festival calendar which developed in this period remained stable for many centuries, despite the cultural upheavals of the Norman Conquest and the Reformation. Festivals like Whitsun may be little known today, but just a few generations ago they still provided the shared communal cycle of holidays in Britain, under names the Anglo-Saxons would have recognised.

In the medieval church, these Christian festivals were just as closely attuned to the seasonal cycle and the agricultural year as the pagan feasts had been. The introduction of a new religion did not change the practical or spiritual needs of this agricultural society: it was still important to pray for and to celebrate a good harvest, to seek divine comfort at the darkest time of winter, and to acknowledge the moment when the longest days of summer moved past their peak. 'Midwinter' and 'Midsummer', the Old English names for the solstices, became transferred to feasts celebrating the births of Christ and of John the Baptist, and for centuries these dates in December and June – the shortest and the longest day – remained significant high points in the English festival year.

For medieval Christians like those of late Anglo-Saxon England, the cycles and rhythms of the natural world and the human relationship with nature were all inextricably connected to a belief in God's role as its creator and sustainer. As they saw it, solar and lunar cycles and the seasons of growth and flourishing in trees and crops all reflected God's power at work in the world; those cycles of waxing and waning, growth and decay, were also mirrored in human lives, connected at the most profound level with our own experience of the passage of time. The lengthening days of spring, for instance, were linked by Anglo-Saxon preachers to the season of renewal and fresh growth which formed the period of preparation for Easter: that was how *lencten*, the usual Old English word for 'spring', gave its name to the Christian season of fasting which we still call 'Lent'. The two meanings are often indistinguishable in Anglo-Saxon sources; *lencten* was a time which suggested both the revival of the earth in spring and the spiritual rebirth of human souls in Lent.

Through links such as these, the new festivals of the Christian calendar became deeply rooted in the English seasonal year, reflecting international customs but adapted to suit the local crops and climatic conditions of the British Isles. This adaptation is especially evident in the season of harvest, with the festival of Lammas, celebrated on 1 August. Lammas may have its origins in a pre-Christian Anglo-Saxon festival; its name, *hlafmæsse*, means 'bread-mass', and it seems to have been a celebration of the first-fruits of the wheat harvest. For the Anglo-Saxons the fourth season of the year, which we would call 'autumn', was simply 'harvest'. A good harvest was essential for sustaining life through the winter months, and harvest was the season when human labour, the fertility of the natural world and the power of God all worked together to bring forth the fruits of the earth. It was, as one poet put it, the season 'most blessed with glory', when divine generosity and the successful produce of long hard work were celebrated with thankfulness.

Once the harvest was in, winter followed hard on its heels. According to Bede, the pagan Anglo-Saxons considered that winter began on the full moon of the month equivalent to October, and for that reason they called the month *Winterfylleð*, 'a name made up of winter and full moon'. Next came *Blotmonað*, 'month of sacrifices', because November was the time when pigs and cattle were slaughtered, and consecrated to the gods, so stores of meat could be preserved to last through the winter. After the conversion to Christianity, this festival became Martinmas, the feast of St Martin of Tours on 11 November, and it long continued to be associated with the killing of livestock. Storing up food for the winter remained an essential need, whatever gods or saints might be petitioned for blessing.

The season of winter, heralded by the full moon of October, could be a real source of fear. Its arrival is described by one poet in violent terms characteristic of Anglo-Saxon writing about winter: it 'seizes sun-bright harvest with its army of ice and snow, fettered with frost by the Lord's command'. Winter is imagined as an invading warrior, a conquering king who sweeps through the earth with the fierce blasts of his snow-army and takes the earth prisoner in his fetters of frost. Such imagery of winter imprisoning or chaining the earth appears across the Old English poetic corpus. It suggests something about the literal restraints winter imposes on human and natural activity: this is the season when bad weather keeps people indoors and stops them from travelling, and the earth can't grow.

In many Anglo-Saxon texts, though, this language is also used to explore other forms of constraint and oppression, psychological as well as physical. These seasons of suffering are what the poet quoted at the beginning meant by writing of every individual's 'share of winters in the world'. That poem, known as *The Wanderer*, is about an exile, grieving for his lost friends as he makes a lonely journey across an icy sea. Amidst the dreary emptiness of this comfortless landscape, he describes himself as *wintercearig*, 'winter-sorrowful', 'as desolate as winter'. The chill of winter has got inside his heart, reflecting the frozen stasis of his sorrow. As he laments his personal grief, he also reflects on loss as a universal part of the human experience. He imagines the world as a ruined hall, its inhabitants slain, beset by the storms of winter:

> Snow falling fetters the earth,
> the tumult of winter. Then dark comes,
> night-shadows deepen; from the north descends
> a fierce hailstorm hostile to men.
> All is full of hardship in this earthly realm…
> Here wealth is fleeting, here friend is fleeting,
> here man is fleeting, here kinsman is fleeting,
> all the foundation of this world turns to waste.

This is an apocalyptic picture; it's as if the whole world's destiny is to succumb to winter, and there's nothing we can do about it.

In normal times, the Anglo-Saxon fear of winter can seem to us like something from another world. Today most of us are disconnected from the natural cycles which were so fundamental to medieval society. We expect food to be available all year round, not only in season, and we don't have to worry about storing enough to help us survive the winter months. We're insulated from the worst of winter's terrors by electric light and artificial heating; we have light at the flick of a switch, so winter darkness doesn't frighten us. This year, though, it doesn't feel quite like that. Disconnected from the natural world, we exploit and damage it, and as a result we're increasingly being reminded what it's like to fear the extremes of heat and cold. This autumn many people, worrying about how they will afford to heat their homes, will indeed be dreading the approach of winter. If, as the Anglo-Saxon poets thought, there's any wisdom to be gained by weathering the difficult winters ahead, it may be in recognising how dependent we are on the well-being of the earth, and how dangerous it is to take that for granted.

Eleanor Parker is Lecturer in Medieval English Literature at the University Oxford and is the author of *Winters in the World: A Journey through the Anglo-Saxon Year.*

Historical Heroes: Mary King of Scots, by Steven Veerapen

Mary Queen of Scots is a figure presented as having a bad choice in men, which led her to flee Scotland and fall victim to her cousin Elizabeth's cunning advisors. As historian and novelist Steven Veerapen states here, she had agency, and ruled not as queen, but as a king and so can justifiably be described as a historical hero.

If asked to envision a British Renaissance warrior-queen, the majority will conjure up images of Elizabeth I. Quite possibly, she will be clad in armour, atop a white horse, one arm raised as she tells an assembled army that whilst she may have the body of a weak and feeble woman, she has the heart and stomach of a king. This is in image we have been fed for years, via Glenda Jackson's star turn in *Elizabeth R*, Cate Blanchett in *Elizabeth: The Golden Age*, and Helen Mirren in *Elizabeth I*. Interestingly, each of these productions have compared Elizabeth – who, we are told, ruled with her head – to her tragic cousin Mary Stuart – who, we are told, ruled with her heart.

The problems here are several. For one thing, contemporary sources do not deck Elizabeth in armour and, for another, there are questions as to which recorded version of her speech she delivered. Further, although Elizabeth could not have known it when she addressed her troops at Tilbury (during the crisis of 1588's Spanish Armada), the naval threat was all but over; a combination of English seamanship and Channel weather had already scattered Philip II's Spaniards. Elizabeth, though her great favourite, Leicester (then in his last days), had forced her into the guise of warrior-queen, was ideologically opposed to English involvement in continental religious war. Her view of armed conflict – especially against sovereign authorities – was as unpopular amongst the Protestant hawks at her court as it was sensible: war was expensive and reaped few rewards. The English queen's preferred methods were subtlety, craft, and avoidance of problems.

Yet, historically, subtlety and craft – usually presented by her critics as duplicitous – have been more associated with Mary Queen of Scots. Conversely, those favourable to the deposed Scottish sovereign have too often sought to present her as a hapless victim: a woman in desperate search of a strong man to help her govern a court of uncouth Scottish nobles, and whose failure to find a decent one resulted in her imprisonment and execution at the hands of such equally nasty figures as the scheming Francis Walsingham and Elizabeth's chief minister, Burghley.

Unfortunately, these competing images of Mary – the serpent queen and the tragic victim – have eclipsed what contemporaries of the queen's personal rule recognised and commented upon: a female sovereign who sought to play the king rather than the queen. It was, in fact, Mary Queen of Scots who was sixteenth-century Britain's active and energetic warrior-queen.

From the outset of her personal rule in Scotland, Mary made it clear that she intended to rule not as a queen but as a king – and a king of Scots. Whilst England's Elizabeth, on acceding as queen regnant, had followed her sister's lead in maintaining the royal bedchamber as a female space, Mary Stuart followed the pattern of Scottish kings: she saw favoured ambassadors in and allowed high-ranking males access to her bedchamber. Nor was she inclined to abandon this performance of male kingship on her remarriage, to the universally disliked Lord Darnley. Too often, in fiction and nonfiction, the Darnley marriage is viewed as a love match, with the fresh-faced young queen falling hopelessly in lust with the 'lang lad'. Yet the match was far from a romance, in its beginning or its end.

As Mary's first cousin, and a young man who had both Tudor and Stuart blood, Darnley was a contender for the English throne, along with Mary, as well as a potential claimant to the Scottish throne. He was, therefore, a rival. Her whirlwind 1565 marriage to the callow youth, far from being a fairy-tale romance, was a calculated political move: in wedding him (almost before he seems to have realised what was happening), she was able to neutralise and – she hoped – subordinate a dynastic rival whilst retaining the Stuart name for any children they might produce. She would name him King Henry – but she intended for him to wear a paper crown, keep out of state affairs, and do his duty as a royal stud horse.

Nevertheless, problems quickly became apparent. As a rebellion (with Mary's chief adviser, her half-brother, Moray, prominent within it) threatened to escalate into civil war, the queen was eager to show her mettle. Mary chose to lead her hastily assembled army in person. As the reformist minister (and enemy to the Crown) John Knox reported, 'The most part waxed weary, yet the queen's courage increased man-like, so much that she was ever at the foremost'. Brandishing a pistol and wearing a steel cap, Mary was keen to fashion herself as a warrior. This was no whim but the satisfaction of a desire she had expressed years previously; during her reduction of the house of Huntly, the English ambassador, Randolph, claimed that she had 'repented nothing … but that she was not a man, to lie all night in the fields or to walk upon the causeway, with a jack and knapsack, a Glasgow buckler, and a broadsword'. The rebels, unwilling to meet their sovereign in open battle, were chased about Scotland and eventually fled to the protection of an exasperated Queen Elizabeth.

All might have been well had Darnley accepted the place his wife had assigned him: a dynastic prize, useful for the provision of heirs. With the rebels banished by their militant queen, Scotland appeared to settle down. Yet 'King Mary' was not contented by her display of 'manlike' fortitude at her army's head. Already she had begun wearing men's breeches under her skirts, and her father-in-law, Lennox, noted her ongoing fondness for male attire. This was not simply dress-up, a young woman's love of masquing – it was the politics of display and performance. Mary was determined that the world should see her as king and queen both. The difficulty was that, in order to provide for the future, she had been obliged to take a king.

That king, however, was far from obliging. The great problem with the Darnley marriage (often problematically blamed on Mary suddenly waking up one morning early in the marriage and realising she had married a fool) was that King Henry, quite naturally for the period, did not expect to be subordinated; he expected to rule. This was anathema to Mary, who by this stage had been governing Scotland well – and in a personal capacity – since her return from France in 1561.

Her response to the nominal King Henry's pretensions was to freeze him out of council meetings and recall the coinage which trumpeted his status. It is sometimes claimed that her actions were due to his unwillingness to engage in state affairs. Yet the opposite is true. Darnley, whose ambition outweighed both his experience and his ability, was *too* willing to assume the reins of power. Evidence here can be found in the memoirs of Lord Herries, who notes that the famous iron stamp the queen had made of Darnley's signature appeared *before* the young king embarked on a lifestyle of hedonistic leisure, not as a result of it. Herries had no reason to sympathise with Darnley, and so his recollections on this point are probably trustworthy. In them, he reveals the source of Mary's dislike of her husband:

The king had done some things and signed papers without the knowledge of the queen … she thought although she had made her husband a partner in the government, she had not given the power absolutely in his hands … [her banished lords] knew [her] spirit would not quit [relinquish] any of her authority, so they addressed themselves to the king … And then, lest the king should be persuaded to pass gifts or any such thing privately, by himself, she appointed all things in that kind should be sealed with a seal, which she gave her secretary David Riccio … with express orders not to put the seal to any paper unless it be first signed with her own hand.

The marriage – between two people vying for the role of king – was doomed. Darnley's sulking despondence made him easy prey for those at the Scottish court unhappy with the power wielded by the foreigner Riccio. In March 1566, disgruntled plotters were able to recruit him in a murderous scheme which saw the unfortunate secretary dragged from the pregnant Mary's supper chamber and stabbed to death.

The consequences of this horrific chapter are well known. Mary was able to convince Darnley of the duplicity of his new friends, and together the pair escaped, regained control despite what was rapidly becoming a palace coup, and the queen was able to be safely delivered of their son, the future James VI and I, in June 1566. Thereafter followed the murky assassination of Darnley at Kirk o' Field in February 1567: an act which followed suspiciously closely on the baptism of James as a Roman Catholic, and which conveniently allowed Mary to be scapegoated as a murderess working in tandem with the Earl of Bothwell.

Mary's great error – the error which can be identified as the beginning of the end of her reign in Scotland – can be reasonably identified as her marriage to Bothwell. The reasons for it defy explanation, although they have been variously portrayed as a genuine love affair, a kidnapping, and, as Mary herself claimed, a 'ravishment' following hard on the heels of her desire – at last – for a man to govern the ungovernable. This claim, on the queen's part, rings false: Mary, as we have seen, was dead against abdicating power to a man. It is possible, of course, that she was so horrified by Darnley's murder – she who always had and always would evince a belief in the sacred nature of monarchy, powerless or otherwise – that she truly did believe Bothwell's promises of being able to bring order to a realm which had shown itself to hold no such belief. More likely, however, is that Bothwell took advantage of a temporary collapse in her mental state and insinuated himself into power – and her bed – with promises of armed, capable support.

The sources, certainly, agree that Mary's behaviour around the time of the Bothwell marriage – those wild and confused days following Darnley's murder – was worthy of note; her celebrated good looks apparently faded and, after the wedding, she called for a knife with which to commit suicide. Yet this, the last of Mary Queen of Scots' marriages, had done damage far greater than her enemies (those who likely aided Bothwell in killing Darnley) could have hoped. They now had what they considered proof that the queen had been, all along, an adulteress and murderess. A hypocritical righteousness (given many had been up their ears in Darnley's death) compelled them to rebel. The newlyweds were chased from Edinburgh and, staying at Borthwick Castle, they parted. Mary's spirit returned. It was reported that she hurled down insults at the besiegers and once again donned male garb, this time disguising herself as a page boy and being lowered from a castle window.

Although they reunited, Bothwell could not provide the support he had promised his wife. Their confrontation with the rebels (still clothed in outraged sensibility) ended in farce; Bothwell rode off on a failed attempt to rally support and Mary was taken prisoner, first at Edinburgh and then at the island fortress of Lochleven. After a traumatic miscarriage and forced abdication, she managed one final great escape, rallied a significant army once again, and clashed with the rebels (now led by Moray) at Langside. When the royal forces were routed, she departed Scotland, anticipating a swift return at the head of an English army provided by her sister-sovereign Elizabeth.

So begins the well-worn twin narratives of Mary the scheming captive and Mary the tragic prisoner. Yet it is notable that, on her arrival in England, Elizabeth's emissary, Sir Francis Knollys, reported that 'This lady and princess is a notable woman. She showeth a great desire to be revenged of her enemies. She showeth a readiness to expose herself to all perils in hope of victory for victory's sake, pain and peril seem pleasant unto her, and in respect of victory, wealth and all things seem to her contemptuous and vile'. Though Mary would never again know freedom, she remained, even in captivity, a captive lion rather than a bound sheep.

Though she is known to history as a victim – whether deserving or undeserving, according to one's biases – it is worth remembering that Mary had, repeatedly and in various ways, sought to rule Scotland as its king. She had dressed the part, acted the part, and even gone so far as to maintain supreme authority despite having taken on a husband. She attempted to, even if finally she could not succeed in, reigning as a warrior.

Steven Veerapen is an academic, historian and author of *Of Blood Descended*, set in the court of Henry VIII.

The Potted Poley, by Peter Tonkin

Tudor courts were teeming with spies, and none is more interesting than Robert Poley. His involvement in the Elizabethan underworld and involvement in many shady events from that period make him a character worthy of study, and of historical fiction.

Tudor courtier, intelligencer and assassin Robert Poley was born in the early 1550s. Queen Mary was on the throne until 1558, so the Poleys, like the rest of the country, were Catholic, though, like many Catholic families, they seem to have remained true to their faith when Protestantism returned with Elizabeth, and so they became recusants. It seemed to some, including Poley, that the only way of avoiding the fines, the stigma and the limitations on employment that recusancy brought with it, was to go underground. The manner in which Poley did this was to become a spy and double-agent.

Nothing is known about Poley's father but his mother probably came from the Blount family, one of whom, Bess Blount, had been Henry VIII's mistress. Nearer Robert's own age were Sir Christopher Blount, also a courier and spy, later husband to Lettice Knollys, Countess of Essex and step-father to the Earl of Essex, executed with his step-son in 1601; and Sir Charles Blount who succeeded Essex in Ireland, ultimately becoming Earl of Devonshire. He may also have been related to Edward Blount who published the first edition of Christopher Marlowe's *Hero and Leander*, and the First Folio of Shakespeare's plays. But it is the spy and the soldier with whom he came most closely associated.

Poley attended Clare College, Cambridge, in 1568 as a sizar, earning his keep as servant to richer students. He did not graduate – suggesting that he remained a Catholic even under Elizabeth's increasingly severe anti-Catholic legislation.

Poley vanishes from the historical record for the next 10 years but his subsequent career suggests he was employed in lowly positions in the household – and later the spy-network - of Sir Francis Walsingham or his relation Sir Thomas (born 1561) as he grew to manhood and assumed some of Sir Francis's network and power.

Poley married (Mary?) Watson in 1580 and their daughter (Anne) was baptised 21st April 1583. The marriage and record of baptism suggest that Poley was at least willing to co-operate with the Protestant authorities. This was a trait which had probably already served him well – and would continue to do so.

By 1583 Poley was seeking employment not only with the Walsinghams but also with the Earl of Leicester. (After Leicester died in 1588, he moved his allegiance to Lord Burghley, and then to his son Robert Cecil.) This initially resulted in nearly two years' incarceration in the Marshalsea jail in Southwark – sometimes under close confinement and at other times with the freedom of the prison. It is generally assumed (as it was at the time) that he was under arrest for his Catholic sympathies but his later work suggests that he was employed as an *agent provocateur*, passing secrets and unwise words from his fellow prisoners straight back to the authorities. (Ben Jonson accused him of doing this; see *Inviting a Friend to Supper*). This supposition would appear to be supported by the fact that Poley was able to mount a mistress while imprisoned (Joan Yeomans, wife of the cutler William), and entertain her to 'many fine banquets'. As in the period before his marriage, he seems to have a suspiciously full purse – especially for a man who had been a lowly sizar at Cambridge.

Poley was released in 1585 and by June he was working with his relative Christopher Blount for the Earl of Leicester. He had stepped up from *agent provocateur*. He was now a trusted courier and secret agent, using his Catholic credentials to take clandestine messages to Paris where he met the Catholic spy-master Thomas Morgan – and so became involved in the outer fringes of the movement to release Mary Queen of Scots from prison, to murder Elizabeth and replace her with Mary, supported by Catholic armies from Italy, Spain and the Low Countries; the so-called Babington Plot.

The success of this mission led to Poley being placed in the household of Sir Philip Sidney who had recently married Frances, the only daughter of Sir Francis Walsingham. Morgan was impressed by this and believed that in Poley he had an agent placed at the heart of the English spy-network. Poley posed as Sidney's man of business but continued to entertain Catholic acquaintances on a lavish scale in his lodgings at Bishopsgate, (which Lord Burghley had set aside for him.) So he moved closer to the heart of the Babington plot – probably under the forger and codebreaker Thomas Phelippes who acted as his 'control' and was in over-all charge of the counter-plot as directed by Sir Francis Walsingham himself.

As Sidney's man of business, there was no need for Poley to accompany his master to the Low Countries in November 1585 but his service in the greater cause was revealed in January of the next year (1586) when Mary's supporters on the continent asked that he arrange for a packet of letters to be delivered to the incarcerated queen. He passed them to Walsingham. Phelippes deciphered them and copied them. Poley sent them onwards – possibly in the false-bottomed beer barrels that were to become such a fatal method of communication between Mary and her supporters. But Elizabeth was not the only subject of Catholic plotting. Poley's position as trusted associate at this time allowed him to get warning of a planned attempt on the life of Leicester himself in May.

But despite Poley's timely warning to the Earl, his cover remained so strong that in June 1586 he was asked to get passports from Walsingham for young Sir Anthony Babington and his companion Thomas Salisbury. In doing so, Poley at last found himself at the very heart of the plot. From that moment on, he became Babington's boon companion (and, some speculate, lover). Certainly, he was soon the idealistic young man's 'Sweet Robyn' and Babington went to his death still refusing to believe Poley to be a traitor and 'of all two-footed creatures the vilest'. In June he entertained almost all of the plotters 'in his garden' (actually the garden of a house specially requisitioned by the government for the purpose). During the following days he briefed Sir Francis and his relative Sir Thomas on the progress of the plot. Babington's letters were opened, decoded (by Phelippes) and passed on. The same was true of Mary's replies the last and most damning of which was six close-written pages long. It fatally agreed to Elizabeth's murder and advised on how best to organise an invasion by Catholic troops from the continent in support of her cause.

When the trap closed, (between 4th and 15th August 1586) Poley was caught along with the rest and spent the next two years in the Tower (no doubt under the same conditions as he had enjoyed in the Marshalsea). Thus, he was behind bars when the Armada was thwarted (May/June 1588) and when the Earl of Leicester died unexpectedly (4th September). His time in prison was given a sinister aspect by the Jesuit Robert Southwell, who accused Poley of murdering Richard Creagh (Catholic Archbishop of Armagh and Primate of All Ireland) by poisoning him with a piece of cheese (at Christmas 1586). Possibly because of this widely-rumoured accusation, Poley's incarceration was not enough to preserve his cover and on his release, he moved onwards – and upwards.

No longer employed as *agent provocateur*, Poley became one of the Privy Council's most trusted couriers from late in 1588 onwards. Almost certainly working with Phelippes, he created nearly unbreakable codes and methods of locking letters to keep them safe. He travelled all over Europe in the pay of councillors such as Sir Francis Walsingham (until his death in 1590, when Sir Thomas succeeded him) Sir Philip Heneage (died 1595) and Lord Burghley until he too died and Poley became chief intelligencer to his younger son the increasingly powerful Robert Cecil.

In the 12 years following his release in December 1588, Poley travelled regularly and widely, to and from Denmark, the Netherlands, France and Scotland. At first glance, Denmark might seem a little out of place until one remembers that James VIth of Scotland was married to Anne of Denmark who, even as Scottish queen, maintained close correspondence with her brother King Christian. And James featured in everyone's calculations more and more forcefully, the nearer the childless Elizabeth came to death.

But on Wednesday, 30th May 1593, Poley stepped briefly out of the shadows into legal and historical limelight because of his involvement in the death of Christopher Marlowe. Marlowe had been a spy since his days at Corpus Christie College Cambridge where he was awarded his BA degree in 1584 but found the university authorities hesitant to award his Master's in 1587 because of his lax attendance. A letter from the Privy Council settled matters in his favour – but seemed to prove that he had been absent from Cambridge on intelligence missions, possibly in the Catholic hotbed of Rheims. Indeed, his absences between 1584 and 1587 together with lavish spending when he was present have led to speculation that he was the 'Morley' who tutored Arbella Stuart, nearest claimant to the throne after James Stuart himself. But all such conjectures are pushed aside by Queen's Coroner Sir William Danby's record of his investigation.

Marlowe (aged 29) spent his last day at Mistress Eleanor Bull's house in Deptford. This was a respectable establishment which let rooms to gentlemen. The gentlemen on this occasion were Christopher Marlowe, Ingram Frizer and Nicholas Skeres, who are usually characterised as minor players in the espionage game. Skeres worked for Essex's spy network, run at the time by the sickly Sir Anthony Bacon. Frizer worked for Sir Thomas Walsingham, and was therefore a rival of Skeres's. It is not clear who Marlowe was working for (Ferdinando Stanley, Lord Strange has been suggested – and he died in mysterious circumstances less than a year later, 16th April 1594) but he was recently returned from Europe under a cloud, was the subject of an arrest warrant and may have been keeping his head down at Scadbury, the house of his literary patron Sir Thomas Walsingham. Poley on the other hand was a senior operative working closely with the most powerful men on the Council, in direct opposition to the others. It all looks like a set-up (see *The Reckoning* Charles Nicholl). They spent the afternoon in quiet conversation. Then an argument exploded between Marlowe and Frizer over who should pay the bill (the 'reckoning'). Frizer was seated with his back to Marlowe who was taking his ease on a bed. Marlowe jumped up, grabbed Fizer's dagger and bashed him over the head with the pommel. Although initially wedged between Poley and Skeres, Frizer was able to turn, snatch back his dagger and stab Marlowe through the eye, driving the blade some two inches straight into his brain. Marlowe apparently died at once and the authorities were summoned. Queen's Coroner Danvers held his post-mortem next day and was convinced by Frizer's plea of self-defence. As was duly recorded, in legal Latin and English.

Whatever his motive for being there, Poley returned to 'business as usual' throughout the late 1590's and early 1600's. He was able to get from London to Edinburgh faster and more reliably than any other courier and there seems little doubt that as Elizabeth's sun began to set, he was employed more and more regularly by Robert Cecil carrying letters to and from King James, thus helping to secure the Scottish succession in 1603.

His last letter to Cecil is dated 18th July 1602, and he seems to have faded from the historical record, aged 50, round about that time. There is ample speculation that he came to a bad end – poetic justice seems to demand it. But there is another possibility under discussion – that, having spent so much time in various prisons for various reasons, he ended his days in the Tower of London. But not as a prisoner this time – as a Yeoman Warder or Beefeater.

Peter Tonkin is a writer and author of The Shadow of the Axe and his latest novel of Elizabethan espionage, The Shadow of the Tower.

Short Story: A Plague on Your Business, by Michael Jecks

The reign of Edward III.

The body was wrapped at last. He had carefully washed her, combing her hair and covering it with a clean linen coif, gently setting her arms at her sides, wiping away his own tears as he worked.

Berenger Fripper had not laid out a body in an age. This was work for women - but in this time of pestilence, all stayed away from corpses. Those who had been touched by the evil buboes must die alone and unshriven. No one wanted to go near in case they might also find themselves afflicted. Some said it was a sign of God's disgust. Berenger knew that was wrong. God could not have wanted to punish his Marguerite. He deserved His justice more. Perhaps this was a punishment for his wrongs?

He picked up the little bundle and placed it carefully on her breast, crossing her arms about it, pressing it tight against her breast.

"There, my love, there. You protect him when you face God together. Keep him with you and … and…"

He could manage no more. Breaking down, he knelt at the side of the table, his brow resting on his dead wife's flank, his hand still on his son's tiny figure, as the hot, angry tears flowed and the sobs threatened to choke him. He was alone again. Never before had he felt such desperate solitude. As a professional soldier, he had enjoyed the comfort and companionship of other men about him, laughing and joking through the good times and the ill but now, since he had taken the offer of a house here in Calais after Edward III had won the city, he was without friends. Old Jacob had died earlier in the week, and his neighbour Fletcher was even now in the last stages of his disease. All those whom he had called friends, he had waved off as they sailed homewards, their purses filled with French gold. Sir John de Sully, Grandarse and his archers, all gone. Not that they would be any safer in England from this disease. Nowhere was safe. God had deserted His people. God was destroying all.

There was a knock and a muffled shout. Berenger wiped his eyes and snorted hard to clear his nose, then made his way out through the little shop to the front door. He opened it to be confronted by a man who stood a wary pace or two away.

'Where?' the man asked. He had a cloth tied about his nose and mouth. It did not prevent the reek of strong wine reaching Berenger's nose. He didn't grudge the man a drink. His was not a job many would wish to take.

Berenger led the way to the parlour where the two lay on his table. He felt another sob from deep in his belly rise up as though to throttle him. It lodged in his throat like a rock, and he could not speak.

The man entered and gazed down at the bodies. 'Your child as well?'

Berenger nodded.

'Godspeed them both, friend,' the collector said and crossed himself.

Berenger busied himself covering her face, once so beautiful, now so empty of feeling and emotion. With the thick needle and waxed twine, he stitched from her feet in great loops that caught the shroud and bunched it up like badly knitted scars. He had to take more twine when he reached her breast, clumsily trying to thread the needle with hands that shook.

'Here, let me,' the carter said, but Berenger snatched his hands away before the man could grab them.

'No!'

This was his wife, and he would see to her remains as best he could. He didn't need another man's help, another man's hands pawing at her.

'Hurry up, eh?' the man said gruffly. He pulled the cloth aside and scratched at his chin before pulling the mask back.

Berenger clenched his jaw, and the thread slipped through the eye. He took up a handful of the shroud and began to stitch. He wouldn't have a stranger getting so close to his Marguerite's breast. It was hateful that the man could see her like this without setting his hands near her. He paused as the needle reached her chin. While he could see her face, he almost felt the life might return to her. Covering her face was the final act. Once hidden, she would be gone forever. He lingered, staring at her, clenching his jaw, willing her to move, to open her eyes, to smile at him ...

But she would not. He steeled himself, and covered her face, stitching quickly as a fresh inundation of tears flooded his cheeks. It was done. She was gone.

The two carried the bundle out to the road to the waiting cart. There were already three bodies lying there: the morning's haul from only a pair of streets. Before the carter reached the end of this roadway, the cart would be full. The wailing and sobbing from all over the city bore testament to the misery of all as carts like this took away their loved ones.

Berenger climbed onto the cart's bed and took his wife and child from the carter. He laid the little parcel down with care, moving another figure to give his wife and child a little more space. Then he clambered down leadenly, and stared as the cart began to clatter off over the cobbles, the figures in the back jerking with every rut and stone as the wheels rattled on.

He was empty. There was nothing in him but a great void. He wanted nothing now; only the oblivion that wine would bring. But he was rooted to the spot, blind to everything but this last glimpse of his wife and child. He watched as the carter stopped a few doors farther along the street, knocking at the timbers, standing aside as two servants brought out the heavy body of Berenger's near-neighbour, Master Richard. The corpulent figure was slumped between them like a sack of turnips and the carter was forced to help them, grabbing the feet while the servants held tight to the shoulders. The men struggled, the carter hauling while the two servants attempted to push the figure up, and Berenger saw the carter stand on his wife's corpse.

He bellowed, and a sudden rage overwhelmed him at the sight of his Marguerite being trampled. His scalp tightened, and he had a clenching in his belly as though a fist was gripping his stomach, and he started to run at the cart. The carter had the winding sheet now, and gripped the dead man's body under the armpits, tugging. One of the servants joined him on the cart, and the two succeeded in lifting the body to sit on the edge. Some of the winding sheet snagged on a splinter or a nail, and the servant below tugged to free it.

It was then that the carter saw Berenger running at him. He cried out to the servants in alarm, before yanking hard at the body. There was a ripping as the corpse's covering tore, and while the servant and carter pushed and shoved, the sheet came away, and Berenger saw the wide-eyed face, the pale features, the loosely moving arms of his neighbour.

The carter turned, knelt on the board and snapped the reins. The horse jerked, began to move while the servant sprang down, and before Bringer could reach the masked carter, he had rumbled his way round the corner.

Berenger ran on a few paces, fuelled by the anger that roiled in his breast, and then, suddenly, he stopped, and almost dropped to the ground as the bitter misery gripped him like an ague.

One of the servants recognised him and stood uncertainly while Berenger covered his face with his hands, trying to get a grip on himself. All he could see was the body of his Marguerite and baby being trampled by the carter.

'Master?'

Berenger glanced at the closed features, the weary, peevish expression of a man impatient with expressions of grief. Everyone had suffered, everyone had lost. What right did Berenger have to indulge himself?

'Leave me!' Berenger snapped, feeling the rage grow. He ran, and when he turned the corner, he saw the cart half-way up the next road. There was a woman in the street, weeping, and the carter had pulled up, dropping from the step like a man sapped of all energy.

In the back of the cart, Berenger saw his neighbour's body resting on top of his wife's. The breath stopped in his breast for a moment, and then he gave an inarticulate bellow and ran straight for the carter. He had no thoughts of his actions, only a blind, unreasoning hatred: for the carter, for the city, for the land which had once seemed so full of promise, and now was filled only with death and destruction. It was as if he was swimming in a sea of blood. All about him was red, raw with rage and hatred.

He didn't even know he was hitting the man until he was pulled away. Panting, struggling to free himself, he stared wide-eyed as the carter was helped up from the ground. He was shaking his head like a dog drying after a dip in a river, blood running from his nose.

'Let him loose,' he said. 'It wasn't his fault. He's lost his family.'

Berenger's arms were released, and he clenched his fists, but only to press them to his eyes as he fought to keep the tears at bay. He had nothing inside him, no more anger. Just this all-consuming emptiness. 'I saw ... you stood on them,' he said brokenly, staring at the corpses in the back of the cart. His Marguerite was still concealed in her winding sheet, but next to her was the merchant. His cold, dead eyes like those of a fish on a slab.

'I lost my mind,' Berenger said. It felt as though a leather strap had been placed about his head, and was tightening as he spoke. Fleeting glimpses of Marguerite kept flashing into his mind; pictures of her laughing, smiling, feeding their son ...

'That man hasn't died from the plague,' one man said.

Berenger glanced at him, then back to the dead Richard.

'There are none of the marks of the plague, no buboes, no stench... he isn't stiff.'

'It takes time for a body to stiffen,' said the carter.

'He died a while ago. Look at him!'

They all knew. They had seen enough corpses, especially in the last couple of years while the English armies ranged over France, and now, with the corpses piling daily.

A man and woman were watching, and Berenger overheard them.

'She won't miss him, you mark my words. Never was there a more brazen hussy. She'll be entertaining her menfolk with pleasure, now that they can visit without risking her cuckold husband's displeasure,' the woman said, short and plump like a hen.

The man was milder. 'Come now, mistress! You cannot seriously believe that! Mistress Alice has lost her husband.'

'I'll bet her purse won't be any the lighter,' the woman said tartly. 'With all her admirers she won't go without!'

'Admirers!' the man scoffed.

'As if you would know! Who would blame her? Master Richard couldn't keep his tarse in his hosen. She told him loud enough for the street to hear that he must throw over his latest wench only last week.'

Berenger rounded on her. He knew the woman. 'You would accuse her, gossip, when her husband is barely cold? You spread malice for no reason other than to bolster your own self-importance,' Berenger snapped. She gasped, and the man with her opened his mouth to remonstrate, but Berenger had heard enough. He turned on his heel and made his way homewards.

It was late in the afternoon that the knock came at his door. Berenger's maidservant had left when Marguerite first began to show symptoms of the disease raging through her body, and he must shift for himself. After years of marching with the King's armies, he was competent to make oatcakes and cook pottage or roast a rabbit, so he did not miss a cook, but he grunted with annoyance when the rap on the timbers came a second time.

'Well?'

Outside stood the carter, unhappily screwing his cap in his hands. Behind him was a man of middle-height, with the broad shoulders and thick neck of a man used to fighting. He stood with his head lowered truculently. 'Berenger Fripper?'

'What of it?'

'I am John of Furnshill, of Sir John de Sully's retinue. I would be grateful for a talk.'

Berenger eyed him for a moment before nodding. Soon they were sitting before his fire.

It was John who spoke. 'You know of the death of your neighbour, Master Richard Allchard?'

'Yes,' Berenger said, giving a cold glance at the carter.

'There have been rumours suggesting that his widow could have been responsible for his death. Do you think that?'

'How should I know? I am a dealer in clothing, not a Keeper of the King's Peace!'

'But you do know her?'

'I have met her.'

'And you were happy enough to defend her name.'

Berenger groaned inwardly. His temper had got the better of him and now it had got him into trouble. 'I heard a woman maligning her, and -'

'And you defended her. There must be a reason for that. You were a soldier once, so I doubt it was a merely altruism on your part.'

'My wife has died. I just … I didn't want to see Mistress Allchard pilloried for something when she's grieving for her husband.'

'Others feel the same,' John said. He stared at Berenger. His eyes were a very dark colour, and under that intense gaze, Berenger grew increasingly uncomfortable. It made him grow choleric, but before he could blurt out an angry remark, the fellow jerked his head towards the carter. 'You saw the body. This man reported it.'

The carter threw a plaintive look at Berenger.

'He had no buboes, and he was coming out of rigor mortis,' John said flatly. 'He did not die of the plague.'

'Perhaps he just didn't show the same symptoms.'

'He had none. He died a little while before, long enough for the rigor to wear off, and then his household kept his body until the carter was coming down the road already. Others say he was murdered. People suspect his widow is guilty. They clamour for her head.'

'Perhaps she did it.'

'Perhaps she did. But Sir John de Sully would not willingly see her pay for another's criminal act. He asked that you should conduct enquiries.'

'Me? Why me?'

John of Furnshill gave a twisted grin. 'Perhaps Sir John feels you still owe him service?'

***

Berenger rapped on the door with his knuckles and stood back. Everyone tried to keep away from others in case the pestilence might migrate from one to another, but Berenger was careless of danger. His wife was dead. Death held no fear for him.

A servant with eyes rather close-set and a thin face opened the door.

'Tell your mistress I would speak with her.'

After a brief delay while the man explained she was in mourning and not seeing visitors, Berenger pushed his foot against the door and shoved it wide. The man squeaked and placed his hand on his dagger, but Berenger quickly grasped his hand and forced it away. An archer's grip is second only to a blacksmith's, and the servant paled as his fingers were crushed like so many pea-pods.

A voice called to him before Berenger could quite break them. 'Master Fripper, I would be glad if you didn't damage my staff.'

Berenger turned, releasing the man, who gave a whimper and clutched his hand to his breast.

She stood in the screens passage, pale and resolute. Waving away her servant, she motioned towards a parlour, and Berenger followed her inside.

Mistress Alice was no beauty. Her face was too round, her eyes too wide-spaced, her mouth too thin, but for all that, there was a vivacity about her that was appealing. Berenger could easily imagine that she would ensnare a lover. Not that she was showing signs of such appeal just now. Her eyes were red-rimmed, as were her nostrils. She had tried to keep her hair beneath her coif, but bedraggled strands dangled. When she tried to smile, she looked like a condemned woman pleading with her hangman.

'Well? What was so important you had to break my servant to speak to me of it?'

'Mistress, it gives me no pleasure to be here.'

'Why are you? Is it to accuse me? You wish to say that everyone thinks I killed poor Richard? That he was murdered by me? I know what the gossips say!'

To Berenger's consternation, she began to weep, her shoulders jerking, although she made no sound.

'Mistress, I am sorry,' he said.

'Everyone is sorry, yet they accuse me. Well, I have not killed anyone, and certainly not my husband. Yes, he took many mistresses, but he always has. Why should I kill him?'

'Perhaps he died of natural causes?' Berenger guessed.

'How can I tell? He began to complain of torment in his bowels, and then writhed on the floor. Nothing we did could help him.'

'His physician …?'

'Master Ashton? You think that sour-faced blood-taker would come to a house hearing someone was unwell, now that the pestilence is here? He refused to visit.'

Berenger had heard of Ashton, a physician who had served in Edward's armies, but whose knowledge was restricted to the mending of bones or phlebotomy. It was not surprising that he would avoid a house with the pestilence. 'Did you explain your husband was suffering?'

'Yes, but he would not come. Richard died and I sat up with him. We called the Coroner, but he said he had no time. No one would come,' she said, and the tears ran without pause.

'Why would people say you killed him?'

'They are jealous? How should I know?'

'Do you have a lover?'

'How can you ask me a question like that?' she spat, but did not deny it.

'Who is he? Others will tell me if you don't,' he said.

She tried to refuse but finally threw up her hands in resentful submission. 'Andrew Peachi, if you must know!'

Berenger had little desire to question Peachi. He had met the man: a vain, fool of some five-and-thirty years. The idea of renewing his acquaintance was not appealing. 'Your husband had no sign of the plague?'

'No.'

'And there was no mark on his flesh? I assume you did search his body?'

'I looked, and so did my steward, but there was no wound.'

'So it must have been something he ate,' Berenger said. 'If there was murder done here, the only means must have been poison. What did he eat that evening?'

'He and I ate the same foods,' she said.

'Which were?'

'We had some Norwegian pasties, meat brewet, a roast of beef, a larded broth, a blankmanger, fresh fruits, and … oh, I can't remember. Speak to the cook.'

***

The cook was a lugubrious, scrawny fellow, like a man who did not enjoy his own food. He was stirring a heavy pottage when Berenger entered the kitchen, and lambasting the kitchen boy for spilling a quantity of gravy.

Seeing Berenger, the cook snarled, 'Get out of my kitchen! I have a meal to prepare, and only a little time to do it!'

'I am here to learn what happened to your master, Cook, and if you don't want it cut from your mouth, you'll keep a civil tongue.'

The man gaped, unused to being threatened in his own place of work, but as Berenger stood and gazed at him truculently, the aggression dribbled away like thin soup through a sieve. He told the kitchen boy to keep stirring his pot and walked to a stool by the table. He poured a cup of weak wine and sipped. 'My apologies, Master, I didn't realise. I'm only a poor cook, when all is said and done. How can I help you?'

'Your master died after eating your food.'

'That wasn't my fault!'

'I am trying to find out what killed him. It may have been an accident. What did he eat that evening?'

It appeared that the merchant had eaten well that evening, it being not a fish day. There were pasties with beef and marrow, Norwegian pasties with cod's livers, a white coney brewet, a roast, a blankmanger … Berenger felt his mind whirl at the list. 'Was there anything that he ate that his wife did not?'

'No. The Norwegian pasties were for Mistress, but they ate everything else.'

'Why were they only for her?'

'She likes them,' he shrugged. 'Master had never eaten them before, so I made them.'

'How did you like your master?'

'Well. He was a good man,' the fellow said. He aimed a kick at the kitchen boy. 'Stir that pottage!'

'What of the rest of the house? Did all think him a good master?'

'Yes. This was a happy house. Although …'

'What?'

The Cook twisted his head in the manner of a man talking of a woman, as though implying carnal knowledge. It was enough to make Berenger want to punch him. He clenched his fist, but kept it at his side. 'Well?' he demanded.

'She has a friend, a man called Peachi,' the Cook said, nodding knowledgeably.

'What do you know of him?'

'Little enough. I am sure he is a pleasant enough fellow,' the Cook leered. He gave a short sound like a snigger. Berenger stepped forward, and would have punched him, but as he moved, there was a loud crash, and then a scream. He whirled about and ran along the passageway, out to the front door.

In the road there was a woman, perhaps mid-twenties, hurling abuse at the house. On seeing Berenger, she picked up a stone from the road and flung it with all her strength at him. He ducked aside and it struck the door-frame and rattled along the flags of the screens passage, Berenger glanced at the house, and saw that she had thrown other stones. One had flown through the window of the hall, and he had no doubt the stone had struck a pot or bowls to make the noise he had heard.

'You killed him, you cow! You foul old hag! You murdered my man, didn't you? Just because you couldn't bear to share him, you decided to tear his heart from him! You ended his life as surely as if you'd used a sword or a dagger!'

There was much more in a similar vein, and she didn't resist when Berenger took her hand and wrested a fresh stone from her grip. 'Come, maid. Where do you live? You cannot stand in the roadway here.'

'Why not? She has murdered him! She must have done!' the woman said, and then her head fell into her hands and she began to sob.

***

He took her to the little tavern at the top of the road. Berenger had visited this place many times with his wife, and it held fond memories. The tavernkeeper, John Barrow, was a great bull of a man, with a moustache that swept back to his ears and a constantly dark jaw where the beard threatened within a half hour of the barber's visit. He had shoulders like a wrestler, and his arms were as thick as young oaks. But now he was diminished. Two months ago he had been the father of four children. Now he had lost all and was widowed. He sat in the corner of the tavern and gazed blearily at Berenger. Berenger served himself from a small barrel of red wine. Dropping coins on the counter, he picked up two cups which he took back to the table where the girl was waiting. Setting the cups before her, he poured from the jug and sat.

'Who are you?' he asked.

'I am Marianne Ashton.'

'Daughter of the physician?'

'What of it?'

'Nothing. I was merely wondering that you began your affair with a man who must have been one of your father's wealthiest clients.'

'He was a kind, good man. I loved poor Richard. Gracious God! I loved him so!'

'How did you meet him?'

'At my father's chamber, paying for his last blood-letting. He was often around when I was at home.'

Berenger could imagine why. Marianne had bright eyes of a greenish colour, and her skin was faultless, smooth and unblemished, with pink flaring at her cheeks. Her neck was as slender as a swan's, her face regular, the mouth full and apparently prone to smiling, from the light creases at either side. She was a lovely woman, and it was all too easy to see that a man like Richard, who Berenger knew had a roving eye, would be entranced.

'But you knew he was married.'

She sniffed, and gulped wine, refilling her cup. 'Of course I knew. But it was a dead marriage. They wed for advantage, but he wanted me for love,' she added, eyes watering. 'She poisoned him. She killed him. She must pay for her treason.'

'Why would she kill him? Was he cruel? Did he beat her?'

'Richard would not have beaten a rabid dog! No, she killed him because she is jealous! She could not bear to think that he might be happy with another. She could not tolerate his choosing someone other than her.'

***

Berenger walked her back to her house.

Before they left, Berenger set the remaining wine in the jug before the tavern-keeper. The man looked grateful, but it was hard to tell. Berenger thought he might return and help the man drink the remaining wine in his cellar. Why not? He craved the oblivion of strong wine.

Her home was the apothecary's shop, a sign declaring that the master here was used to dealing with the English. Any tradesman had to declare that, since the siege and the capture of the town by King Edward III. Berenger rapped on the timbers of the door.

The man who opened it was tall and lugubrious, with mournful eyes. He looked from Berenger to Marianne and back, and he seemed to shrivel at the sight. 'Who are you? What do you want?'

'My name is Berenger Fripper, and I brought her home before she could be arrested for lobbing stones at another woman's house.'

'Oh, Marianne, what now?' the man groaned.

'She killed him, father. You know that as well as I.'

'I know nothing of the sort. Friend, Master Fripper, I am glad you brought her home. You have my gratitude. And now …' he turned, beckoning his daughter in to join him.

'One moment, Physician. Why did you not go when Mistress Alice called you? She said her husband was unwell, but you did not go to him.'

'I was engaged with another client. I could not go. Have you not noticed that the pestilence is all about you? It is here in the air. Every breath you take out of doors will see you succumb the sooner, especially at night when it is most virulent. I could not think of going to him then. And I was with another client.'

'Which client?'

'That is none of your business,' the man said. He held Berenger's gaze as he slowly pulled the door closed.

The sound of bolts sliding home came to Berenger. 'You, master, are lying,' he murmured.

***

Andrew Peachi was a slim, elegant man in his middle thirties, a man nearer to Alice's age than her husband had been. Peachi was round-faced, but with a lively sparkle in his eyes that spoke of his adventurous nature.

He smiled when Berenger entered his house. 'Master Fripper, I think? We have met before.'

'Yes, Master Peachi. At the house of Sir John de Sully. You were there with a fresh conquest.'

'Conquest?'

'I've known many men treat women as toys to be played with and then discarded. Beatrice of Sens was infatuated with you until her death. Was it because of you she died?'

Peachi's smile fell away and he grew sorrowful. 'That was a terrible thing. They say that she slipped while she was walking along the quayside.'

'They often say such things to save the poor and afflicted from being accused of self-murder,' Berenger said.

His words unsettled Peachi. 'Some women cannot accept that they have become superseded. I fear that Beatrice was sweet, very sweet, but not very mature. She was little better than a child.'

'You took advantage of her and that led to her self-killing.'

'Oh, really!' he waved a hand airily. 'She couldn't understand when our relationship was over. It was clear enough that there was no more for us. She wanted to continue, but, what could I say? It was too late.'

'Because you had another woman lined up: Alice.'

'I wouldn't -'

'She has already told me that she was having an affair with you,' Berenger said.

A smile crossed Peachi's face. Another conquest; another addition to his reputation.

Berenger nodded. 'So you had a desire to see her husband removed.'

The smile fled from his face like quicksilver from a tilted bowl. 'You cannot mean that.'

'You wanted her; you wanted the freedom to take her whenever you wanted; you wanted the risk of her husband removed. It must have been galling, taking on a married woman - not a young wench you could easily pursue, but a woman who was unfree and married. You must have seen her as a more inspiring challenge - but then - what? You decided you wanted her entirely for yourself? You could not bear to share her with another? A situation easily resolved with poison in her husband's food. Much safer than stabbing him in the street, much safer than risking yourself. Did you bribe the cook?'

Peachi shook his head. 'Challenge? Yes, she was a challenge, but less difficult than she might have been. Richard's womanising was flagrant, and he rubbed her face in his conquests all too often. She was a willing partner, for a while. But she still loved him. She told me it was over. You think I killed him? I know nothing about poisons, and I know no one in the house apart from her! If someone killed her husband, it must have been she herself!'

'I will be sure to tell her that is what you believe.'

'Do so! You think I'd live with a woman who could murder her own husband?' the man sneered.

Berenger rose. 'So you will not support her now?'

'You think me a fool? Everyone would be sure to comment on my relationship with her!'

Berenger nodded, and then his fist lashed out. He caught Peachi below the rib-cage, and the fellow bent almost double as the air whooshed from him, and then Berenger hit the side of his head and the man collapsed. A kick to his cods left him gasping, clutching at his damaged privates, rolling on the stone floor.

'If I hear you've tried to pin cuckold's horns on another man, I will castrate you,' he said, and left the room.

***

He returned to the tavern. John Barrow was still in his corner, but now there were three jugs on the floor about him, and he was weeping inconsolably. Berenger poured him more wine and sat beside him with his own cup. It was growing dark outside, and in a few moments John passed out, his head against the wall, his mouth wide, snoring a rasping, dirge-like tune that rose and fell, rose and fell.

Berenger drank cup after cup, but his mind would not rest. He saw his wife and child: Marianne smiling and happy, laughing; naked in the candle light that brought a golden glow to her body; in the river, her sleeves rolled up as she beat the clothes clean in the river's water; cooking, pushing the hair from her face as she perspired over the oven or brew pots ... then pale and dead as he sewed the last stitches in her winding sheet.

Suddenly something struck him: a cook making little pasties ... if they had been made for Allchard, it would have been easy to see who was guilty of the murder. But these were Alice Allchard's favourite ...

He stood and shivered. Leaving the tavern, he walked homewards and fell into his bed. Waking in the middle of the night, he threw his hand out, but it encountered only cold sheets. He sobbed then, until sleep took him once more. Never had he felt so alone.

**

The next morning, he woke, thrust his head into the trough before his house, and made his way back to the widow's house.

Alice was seated in her hall when he entered. 'Mistress, your chef told me that he made pasties for you because your husband didn't like them.'

'He did? He made the pasties because he knows they are my favourite dainties, but I had none. My husband had never tried them, but he found they were to his taste, and ate them all. I was happy he enjoyed them.'

Berenger nodded slowly. The cook had made the pasties for her, and her husband had eaten them. Were they poisoned? The idea that had formed in his mind the previous night came back in full force. He asked for the cook to be brought to him.

The man was pale and sweat glistened on his brow. 'Well?'

'Who told you to make those pasties?'

The man shiftily glanced at his mistress. 'I –'

'Look at me! Who suggested them?'

'The master.'

'He had not tried them. You said they were dainties for Mistress Alice.'

'They were! He knew she loved them!'

'Yet he ate them all.'

'I ... He must have discovered he liked them too.'

'A man who asks for a treat for his wife would hardly be so crass as to eat it himself and deprive her. Who told you to make them?'

'My sister!'

'Your sister?'

'Yes.'

**

It took little effort to have him confess after that, and soon Berenger was outside the physician's house with John of Furnshill.

'I hope you are correct, Master Fripper.'

'If you don't trust my judgement, go and tell Sir John that I have failed,' Berenger snapped and knocked.

There was a brief interval while both men stood waiting. When the door opened, Berenger was shocked to see the pale, drawn expression on the face of the maid. 'What has happened?'

'The poor little chit! The poor thing!' the maid said.

They found Ashton in his parlour, cradling his daughter's body. He looked up with raw eyes that flamed at the sight of Berenger. 'This is your doing!'

'What has happened?' John of Furnshill demanded.

'She was distraught at poor Master Allchard's death. So distressed ...'

'No,' Berenger said. He walked to the table and sat.

'Why? What do you say?'

'This: your daughter planned to kill Mistress Alice. She learned of a tempting dainty that Alice would eat, and persuaded her brother, your son and the Allchards' cook, to add something. I doubt he knew what it was, but afterwards he realised. As you did. Was it something missing from your stores? She took poison and your son unwittingly killed his master. Because his master suddenly learned that he liked this new dainty, and his wife, enjoying his pleasure, willingly allowed him to finish it. That was why your daughter yesterday accused Alice of murder, because Alice should have eaten them all herself. Instead, Marianne discovered that her plan had killed her lover. As you knew. That was why you chose not to visit the house to see Richard's death throes.'

'I guessed. How could I have guessed? It never occurred to me that Marianne could have thought to do such a thing. And it was her lover whom she killed, not her rival. And now I have lost her!'

'She is little loss to you,' John said flatly as he stood again. 'But justice has been served.'

'Surely there is no need to tell anyone? She died in her sleep, and it was an accident.'

Berenger answered: 'She took her own life from despair after realising she had slain her lover. If her guilt is concealed, Alice will suffer. She is the only innocent in this sad affair. So no, Marianne's guilt will not be concealed, nor will her self-murder.'

'You would threaten her soul? She is dead, Master Fripper! Show mercy!'

'I give you respect for your loss, but mercy for her? She murdered a man, meaning to kill another from jealousy and greed. My concern lies with the living.'

***

They walked out a little later, the pair of them silent. In the street they saw another collector's cart laden with the dead, and the two averted their faces as it passed.

'I am grateful to you for your help,' John of Furnshill said.

'It is nothing.'

'What will you do now?'

Berenger considered the question. He thought of his house, now so empty; of Alice and her husband; of Marianne and her brother; and finally of the tavern - but he said nothing.

'Why did Sir John de Sully ask me to investigate?'

'Why do you think?'

'I can only think because he wanted Alice to be free of suspicion. Perhaps he knew her husband? Or, perhaps he knew her and did not want her to be maligned?'

'Sir John is not young. When he was a youth, he met a woman, and had a daughter. I doubt many men would wish to see their children accused of murder.'

ASPECTS OF HISTORY

Michael Jecks is the author of *The Vintener Trilogy*, the latest of which is *Blood of the Innocents.*

His Own Messenger: The Rise of Cyrus the Great, by Matt Waters

The Achaemenid Empire was the greatest the world had ever seen, spanning from the Greek cities on the coast of Asia Minor to the mountains of Afghanistan. Its founder was Cyrus, a ruler whose achievements made him truly 'Great'.

Shortly after Cyrus the Great conquered the Babylonian Empire in 539 BC, he dedicated inscriptions commemorating his achievements, to wit: "The great gods have delivered into my hands all the lands, and I caused the land to live in peace." With much of the known world under his rule, it was not far from a literal truth. The question remains how Cyrus accomplished this so effectively, and so quickly. Among his other attributes, speed and decisiveness are often noted: in several instances Cyrus seized the initiative against his enemies so rapidly that he often arrived, ready for battle, as his own messenger. The empire that Cyrus founded in just over a decade reached from Central Asia to the Aegean Sea. Within the next generation Cyrus' successors added Egypt, Libya, and the Sudan; the Indus Valley; as well as parts of the Balkans and south-eastern Europe. It was far and away the largest empire to date and persisted in its essentials for two hundred years, only superseded, and then for less than a decade, by Alexander of Macedon's conquest of it. Cyrus has not received the attention that one might expect for a ruler of such import and such lasting impact.

The most important royal inscription extant from Cyrus himself is the famous Cyrus Cylinder from Babylon. Therein, Cyrus' traced his royal lineage through three generations to his great-grandfather Teispes as kings of Anshan. Anshan was the age-old name given by the Elamites, the Persians' predecessors in Iran, to the region called subsequently Parsa (modern Fars), the core of the Achaemenid Persian Empire. About Teispes we know little beyond the name, though there are glimpses in mid-seventh century Assyrian sources of a Persian kingdom on the rise, probably under his rulership or that of his son, the first Cyrus. (Cyrus the Great was Cyrus II.) Cyrus the Great's father, Cambyses I is also a bit of a cipher. He is attested as Cyrus' father in royal inscriptions from Babylonia, but even in Greek narrative sources he is not much more than a genealogical reference point. Detailed information about Cyrus' life and other aspects of his career survives primarily from a mixed bag of Greek and Roman accounts that date a century or more after Cyrus' death. These later accounts contain a rich trove of embellished material: historical narrative; didactic literature; and the authors' plays on, often subversions of, Persian royal ideology as received in the provinces.

The three main Greek sources give fundamentally different accounts about Cyrus. These writers, in chronological order from the later fifth into the mid-fourth centuries BC, were

Herodotus, Ctesias, and Xenophon. Herodotus explicitly noted that he knew of four different accounts about Cyrus; if Herodotus' given version is the least exaggerated among the four that he knew, one wonders what the others contained. The version about Cyrus' youth that Herodotus chose to relay stems from a tradition of which the main purpose was to legitimize Cyrus in the Median dynastic line. In this version Cyrus was grandson of the last Median king Astyages. Ctesias of Cnidus, writing c. 400 BC, also linked Cyrus to the Median dynastic line, but by way of marriage to Astyages' daughter, named Amytis in that tradition, after Cyrus' victory over her father. Despite the divergence in details in Herodotus' and Ctesias' accounts, the versions therein are both renderings of the so-called Sargon Legend, named after Sargon of Akkad of the twenty-third century – the tale of the hero exposed at birth, or alternatively of humble upbringing, beloved and chosen by the gods, who achieved his destiny of kingship – the theme also famously applied to Moses, Oedipus, Romulus and Remus, among others.

Cyrus was driven, relentless, and a perceptive commander. He campaigned across the ancient Middle East, parts of Central Asia, and through most of Anatolia, and seemingly none could withstand him. His military career was remarkable in its own right, and particularly so when juxtaposed with the scope and scale of territories that now came under one rule, unprecedented to that point in history. The three most celebrated conquests were over the premier powers of the day and dated from the late 550s through 539: the Medes in northern Iran, the wealthy Lydian kingdom in Anatolia, and the Babylonian Empire. The Medes were a key factor in the overthrow of the Assyrian Empire in the 610s, working in conjunction with the Babylonians to bring down the foremost power of that era. It is not clear how long this teamwork continued. The last Babylonian king, Nabonidus (reigned 556-539), himself ultimately a target of Cyrus, made no hesitation to throw the Medes under the chariot as somehow responsible – the "somehow" is never precisely delineated – for the shabby state of several temples in northern Mesopotamia. The Medes were thus blocking Nabonidus' big reconstruction plans. The chief Babylonian god, Marduk, assured Nabonidus in a dream not to worry. The Medes then became the villain, colourfully labelled as the *umman-manda*, an age-old Babylonian-language pejorative for barbarians, as relayed in one of Nabonidus' inscriptions from the late 550s.

> "The *umman-manda* of whom you speak, he, his land, and the kings
> who go at his side, are no longer a threat." In the third year, the gods
> caused to rise Cyrus, the king of Anshan…

This inscription contains the first attested reference to Cyrus the Great, introduced as the divine agent who overthrew the Babylonians' main rivals, those enemies of the gods. the Medes.

Greek authors had a lot to say about Cyrus' conquest of Lydia, ruled by the proverbial, "rich as" Croesus. Greek interest in Lydia was not surprising; western Anatolia was closer to home and for many Greeks it was home, an area that was subject to Lydia before the Persian conquest. Herodotus, in typical Greek literary form, cast Croesus' gambit against Cyrus as the epitome of hubris: the misinterpretation of an omen and the desire to augment his own territory. When Croesus asked the oracle at Delphi whether he should attack Cyrus, the response came that if he did so he would destroy a mighty empire. But it was Cyrus who defeated him, and the mighty empire Croesus thus destroyed was his own. Croesus departed to engage Cyrus and, after an inconclusive battle, withdrew to his capital, Sardis, to await the Spring and reinforcements. Cyrus, however, unexpectedly stole a march and "came as his own messenger to Croesus" before any reinforcements could arrive. Cyrus nullified Croesus' cavalry through a ploy that involved positioning at the front of his forces pack-camels, from which the Lydian horses fled. Overcome, the Lydians were besieged until a Persian force climbed a supposedly-unassailable cliff to access the city. Already victor over the mighty Medes, once Cyrus vanquished the Lydian resistance, he became certainly much "richer than Croesus."

Greek authors did not provide much detail on the conquest of Babylon, probably because they knew little about it. In Herodotus' account, the great city was taken after a short siege of a supposedly impenetrable wall, an echo of the taking of Sardis. Herodotus made a point, however, to devote some time to Cyrus' diverting two rivers during the Babylonian campaign, as this allowed Herodotus to dwell on one of his favourite themes: the Persian kings' hubris manifest by their transgressions of rivers and other natural boundaries. This sets the stage for Cyrus' later crossing of the Araxes, for Darius I's crossing of the Bosporus, and Xerxes' even more infamous crossing of the Hellespont en route to punish Athens and conquer Greece.

On the other hand, ancient Near Eastern sources supply a mine of information for the conquest of Babylonia and the Levant and its aftermath. Thousands of surviving archival texts attest to the administrative organization of the Persian imperial apparatus there, which, at least for the first few decades of Persian rule, understandably adopted the Babylonian system that it inherited, in turn based on the Assyrian model. The Babylonians had presumably watched with unease as Cyrus conquered vast swaths of territory to his east, north, and northwest. Nabonidus attempted to forestall Cyrus' advance, but his preparations came to naught. A major battle was fought at the city of Opis, near modern Baghdad, in early October of 539 BC, which paved the way for Nabonidus' capture, an orderly transition, and Cyrus' ceremonial entry into Babylon later that month. The Cyrus Cylinder, alluded to earlier, is a paean to Cyrus and a testament to his observance of proper rites and norms. While it contains many innovations in its composition and style, it also is a traditional Mesopotamian royal inscription. In lyrical terms it vilifies Nabonidus and trumpets Cyrus' own legitimacy. And the emphasis turns on a key point: Cyrus was chosen by Marduk to put a stop to the outrages: the divinely-selected king who will correct previous wrongs and reinstitute proper forms was an age-old theme in Mesopotamia. "Marduk surveyed and considered all the lands, he searched thoroughly for a just ruler, one favored in his heart. Marduk took him by the hand, Cyrus, the King of Anshan, he summoned his chosen one, he named his name to rule over all."

The text also refers to the return of gods to their sanctuaries and of peoples to their settlements. The specific places mentioned were located along a (if not "the") most important route from Susa through the Elamite-Babylonian borderlands, a contested area among regional powers for centuries previous and, for that matter, through the Iran-Iraq war during the 1980s in the modern period. While not specifically mentioned in the Cylinder's list, the same magnanimity was accorded to the Judeans. This resulted in the most well-known consequence of Cyrus' act, the end of the so-called Babylonian Diaspora: the deportation of Jewish population to Babylonia after Nebuchadnezzar II's sack of Jerusalem in 587/86. It is thus no surprise that Cyrus is lionized in the Hebrew Bible – positive press follows him in almost every tradition – the Book of Ezra credits Cyrus for the restoration of the temple of Jerusalem. Cyrus was literally termed a messiah, "the anointed" in the book of Isaiah, "…(The Lord) who says of Cyrus, 'He is my shepherd, and he shall fulfil all my purpose'" and "… Cyrus, whose right hand I have grasped to subdue nations before him…" Cyrus' magnanimity in releasing subject peoples and their gods served as the pivot point for a renewal of local traditions in Judah and elsewhere. It was also a shrewd strategic move that afforded Cyrus the opportunity of loyal subjects throughout Greater Mesopotamia and the Levant. We must allow for the likelihood that Cyrus had his sights upon Egypt as well, but the conquest of much of north-eastern Africa fell to his son and successor, Cambyses II. Cyrus died in August of 530 BC, on campaign somewhere east of the Aral Sea. He left an indelible legacy, and his successors continued his work, which included his new capital, Pasargadae, a foundational tribute to the Persians' renowned love of gardens as well as a physical manifestation of the first universal empire.

Matthew Waters is Professor of Classics and Ancient History, the University of Wisconsin-Eau Claire and the author of *King of the World: The Life of Cyrus the Great.*

The First Tycoon, by Peter Stothard

Marcus Crassus is not a likeable character of ancient Rome. The most prominent figure in the pre-Caesarian era, he was played brilliantly, and rather sleazily, by Laurence Olivier in the film, Spartacus. In his new book, Peter Stothard has written about a man who was fabulously wealthy, but who inevitably flew too close to the sun.

Marcus Licinius Crassus was famous for a boast. No one should be considered rich, said the richest Roman of his time, unless he could finance an army from his own income. Twice he lived up to that boast, the first time against Spartacus gaining himself only ingratitude, the second time beside the Euphrates costing his life and a national humiliation.

The man who I call 'The First Tycoon' was not content with being massively rich. Crassus was a money-man in the age of more conventionally successful men, Julius Caesar and Pompey the Great, a pioneering banker who wanted also to match Rome's greatest generals as a man of war. He was a long-time rival of Pompey and financier of Caesar (in many ways he had created him) but at the end of his life he wanted military glory of his own.

Crassus was a balancer of power at a time of savage instability, playing his fellow citizens against their rivals, big and small. In 53 BCE he had for thirty years worked innovatively behind the scenes of the political stage at Rome but his last and most lasting legacy was of his own severed head, stuffed with gold, as a prop in a tragic theatre thousands of miles away.

Crassus's life was a classic tragedy of rise and fall. The first tycoon of ancient Rome would be remembered as its most famous loser. If he had died in 54 BCE he might have quietly entered history as Rome's richest man, its first modern financier and political fixer, the brutal suppressor of Spartacus's slave rebellion and a respected colleague of Caesar and Pompey at the pinnacle of power in Rome's collapsing republic. His modern face would have been from 1960, Laurence Olivier in Stanley Kubrick's Spartacus.

Instead, in 53 BCE, he led his banker's army on an unprovoked campaign against the Parthian empire into what are now the borderlands of Turkey, Syria, and Iraq. He lost a desert battle and the eagle standards of his legions near a small town called Carrhae. His head was said to have been filled with molten gold and used in a Greek tragedy when the plot required the remains of an arrogant king. The legacy of Crassus was a peculiarly catastrophic defeat that took a potent hold on the Roman mind.

Crassus was no ordinary failure, just as he had been no ordinary success - a man whose life as businessman and politician posed both immediate and lasting questions about the intertwining of money, ambition, and power. It is hard to write about him now and not think of Vladimir Putin, drawn to continuing disaster in Ukraine, for whom a legacy as a multi-billionaire ruler of Russia was not enough – and only matching Stalin or the greatest Tsars will do.

Crassus's fortune came from exploiting the end of the civil wars in which he had lost his father and brother. From soon after his birth in 115 BCE, fifteen years before Caesar's, his life was marked by the sight of heads on spikes as radicals and conservatives fought for power at Rome. In 83 BCE he had his best military success as an officer for the soon-to-be dictator, Lucius Cornelius Sulla. A messy triumph at the so-called Battle of the Colline Gate brought him the opportunity to buy the lands of the defeated and 'proscribed', to apply his own radical techniques of insurance and moneylending. Crassus was a subtle avenger. While others repaid past debts in blood, he bound thousands to him in getting and spending.

His getting was at first from the misfortunes of Sulla's enemies, the spending, throughout his life, on those who might take their place in the power structures of Rome. His regular critic, the orator Marcus Tullius Cicero, likened the getting to a harvest; the spending was like the distribution of free food to the poor, an investment in gratitude. Crassus was an innovator at both, not least in living a comparatively modest life himself, despising the would-be rich who borrowed to buy their big houses, living in a single house at Romer with a wife who was his brother's widow and two sons, one of whom joined him on the fatal journey to Carrhae.

His successful leadership of an army against Spartacus, an escaped gladiator who had extraordinarily become a threat to Rome, was an opportunity that came thirteen years after his victory at the Colline Gate. It was not, however, one that he, or any other potential commander, much relished. Pompey and Caesar were conveniently away when the crisis came. There would, they all knew, be no glory in defeating an army of slaves whom the Romans did not deign even to call an army. There could be no triumph, no applause in the streets, after a war which was not a war. Failure, on the other hand (and two allies of Pompey had already failed) would be the end for Crassus.

There was dangerously little cash in the state Treasury at the time. Crassus was the man who could raise, train and equip an army from his own resources. His property empire was as useful a training ground as any part of a foreign empire. He employed tens of thousands of slaves and recognised what, with good leadership, they could achieve. He respected Spartacus as others had not.

Crassus successfully crushed the rebellion, using his skills of organisation as much as any other. It was then his choice how to treat the prisoners who, unlike Spartacus himself, had survived the last battle. The long line of crucifixions between Capua, where the original escape took place, and the start of the Appian Way at the walls of Rome became the symbol by which two thousand years later Crassus would be most remembered. In 70 BCE it was a horror that Romans wanted as quickly as possible to forget.

There was, as he expected, no Triumph, merely a lesser honour, slightly enhanced by negotiation, in return for his huge investment of financial and political capital. Pompey even claimed a share of such honour that there was by mopping up a few rebel stragglers as he returned from Spain. Crassus could soon see Pompey and Caesar, with new wealth from conquest, as increasingly likely to exceed his influence at Rome. He himself remained far behind their reputations as conquerors.

Gradually the stage was set for what would become the fatal assault on Parthia. Crassus joined his rivals in an informal triumvirate that critics called the 'Three-Headed Monster'. Each man had his own space in which to advance his ambitions without fear of hindrance by the others.

Parthia was a faraway land of which few Romans knew anything. It began in borderless zones east of the Euphrates and stretched without fixed end towards China. It was reputedly rich and prosperous; its barbarian rulers were members of a single fratricidal family; and the military intelligence available even to Crassus, the meticulous planner, was not much more than that. The idea of a Roman conquest was not new but there were plenty of nay-sayers (especially Cicero) and soothsayers (especially when the catastrophe at Carrhae had happened) who advised (or said that they advised) that the invasion plan should remain unused.

Crassus could not be dissuaded. He could afford his own army. His place at the top table of politics depended on its use. Caesar allowed Crassus's son, who was serving heroically as a cavalry officer in Gaul, to bring horsemen for the Parthia force. Crassus planned and he drilled but he had little idea what he was preparing for or whom he would be fighting.

His humiliation was not inevitable. Like Vladimir Putin today, he was unlucky in his adversary. He might have expected to face a cynical elder of the Parthian royal family who would skirmish, retreat, cede territory, do a financial deal and wait to return when the Romans had tired and gone. Ukraine too had many would-be and has-been leaders of that sort from the Soviet era.

Instead he came up against a young and charismatic general called Surenas, the Zelensky of the desert one might say, who had a determination to defeat the Romans and his own innovative ways of doing so. In what became a compelling story for those who survived to tell it, Crassus entered a trap in which archers and armoured horsemen, with no infantry to match his legions, destroyed an army in direct contravention of every rule of Roman war.

The humble camel, not a beast much known to Crassus's army, was deployed for reloading arrows in such a way as to turn every bow into an AK47. The deadly missiles came and kept on coming. Every legionary eagle standard was lost. Crassus saw the head of his son on a spike before dying himself in a desperate attempt to talk terms. Crassus's own head was severed and taken back, with the eagles, to the Parthian king.

The barbarian court, or so it was said, was at the time of its arrival watching a performance of Euripides's great Greek tragedy, *The Bacchae* (not a play ever performed for the proudly civilised of Rome) and the head of Crassus became a perfect stage prop for the scene when an arrogant king is torn apart by his mother's maddened female band. In some versions its mouth was stuffed with molten gold. A look-alike Crassus was paraded in the closest approximation to a Roman triumph that the Parthians could produce.

Peter Stothard is the author of *The Last Assassin: The Hunt for the Killers of Julius Caesar* and *Crassus: The First Tycoon.*

Who was Agricola? By Simon Turney

Agricola, to those who have heard the name, will know it is familiar to Roman Britain, but that's probably about it. Using archaeological evidence, along with Tacitus' account, Simon Turney has painted a vivid picture of a man who learnt his trade fighting Boudicca, but who left his mark.

The son of a minor nobleman of Gallic birth with a fascination over viticulture, Gnaeus Julius Agricola climbed the ladder of Roman political offices like others of his era, so why is he so important to Roman Britain? Quite simply from the day Julius Caesar landed an exploratory fleet in Kent in 55 BC to the day the empire told Britain to "look to its own defence" in AD 410, no Roman was more involved in shaping the island's history than Agricola.

At various points in the course of a political career, a Roman of the equestrian or patrician classes would serve in certain roles or posts. The first was that of a military tribune, the equivalent of an untrained commissioned officer serving over the centurions but under the legion's commander where they might be used for logistical purposes or to relay commands etc. Later in a man's career, he would command a legion as its legatus. He would also serve as a governor of a province, at least once if not twice.

Where Agricola is unusual is that he served many of his major postings in the same province. As well as a questorship in Asia and a minor gubernatorial role in Aquitania, he spent the three aforementioned roles all in Britain, and perhaps made more out of those positions than most did.

As I already intimated, the junior tribune was usually a political appointee, a young and inexperienced noble just enduring a two-year posting in order to secure a better political post, a sort of upper-class National Service in ancient Rome. Agricola received his posting in Britain. There may be a number of reasons for this. There is good reason to presume a connection between his family and those of the Flavii and the Plautii, both of whom had been involved in the initial conquest of Britain less than two decades earlier. Familial connections were a common method of securing position, and Agricola would be no stranger to this. We do not know to what legion Agricola was sent, but there is good reason to believe it was the 2nd Augusta in Exeter. Tacitus tells us that Agricola was taken into the command staff of the governor on his arrival, and so from AD 58 to AD 60, Agricola stomped around the hills and valleys of Wales with the army of Suetonius Paulinus. As such he would have been involved in the first attacks on Anglesey. But more importantly he would have been involved in the war that dragged the governor back from Wales. A certain redhead over in East Anglia by the name of Boudicca rose with her tribe and burned three cities. Agricola would have been with the army that raced south and east and brought the wronged queen of the Iceni to battle on Watling Street. In that campaign and its aftermath, he would have also made new and important imperial contacts, including Titus, son of the future emperor Vespasian, and Petilius Cerialis, son in law of the same emperor.

After a brief sojourn in Asia, Agricola proved himself a close friend of the Flavian family during their meteoric rise to power during the year of the four emperors, along with Ceralis who he'd met in Britannia. He was given a minor role in raising troops, and then, once Vespasian was settled, given a new task. Cerialis was to be assigned as governor of Britain, but one of the legions on the island was rebelling, and had been since the time of the previous governor. Agricola was therefore made commander of the Twentieth Valeria Victrix in Chester, and sent back to Britain for a second stint. Arriving on the island, he seems to have essentially settled the legion with a mix of stern admonishment and accepting reason. A sort of 'we all know what you did, but pull yourselves together and we'll never speak of this again.' It worked, perhaps because he was already a wartime veteran of the island, and probably already knew important men in the army. Once the Civilis revolt in Germany was settled, Cerialis arrived and he and Agricola set about the conquest of the North. Wales being now largely settled, the two men formed a two-pronged attack on the Brigantes, the largest tribe in England. In a few short years the two soldiers had the Brigantes surrounded, suppressed, and beginning the process of Romanisation. In 73, Agricola is recalled, sent to govern Aquitania, and the conquest of Britain takes a breather. In fairness, the governors that followed did, in fact, apparently advance the cause somewhat, but our focus is on Agricola, so we should note that he has now fulfilled both military roles on the ladder in the same province, overcoming some of the most powerful tribes on the island and exploring the frontier regions both times.

After a time in France, then, Agricola is made consul, granting him access to the more powerful and important provinces. It should be little surprise that Vespasian, emperor of Rome, family friend of Agricola and veteran of the British invasion, sends Agricola in AD 77/78 to take on the governorship of the island. Likely Agricola is given the remit "finish the conquest." Agricola is governor of Britain under the aegis of all three of the Flavian emperors, Vespasian, Titus and Domitian, between then and 83. Agricola has been a tribune and a legate in Britain, a governor in Aquitania, and a questor in Asia, and puts into play everything he learned in all those years. The conquest of Britain would be completed by probably the only man who had ever spent most of his career, a quarter of his life, on the island.

The Roman border was now along the line of the Tyne/Solway isthmus. Arriving in AD 77, Agricola puts down a rebellion in North Wales and invades Anglesey yet again. With Wales finally under control, in 78 he takes control of the northern corridor, the Cheviots, the territory of the Selgovae, and likely takes the peaceful annexation of Northumberland. In 79 he advances across the Tay and consolidates on the Gask Ridge, taking the Roman border ever northward. In 80, the consolidation of currently held territory continues, and in 81 the area of Dumfries and Galloway is taken under control, with Agricola even contemplating an invasion of Ireland, an exiled Irish prince in his retinue. Then in 82 there are disasters, northern campaigns, and a general push towards the Highlands. With the arrival of 83, he finally manages to force the remaining tribes of the Highlands, the confederation of the Caledonii, to meet him in battle at a place Tacitus calls Mons Graupius, probably the hill of Bennachie. There, a great, climactic battle sees Agricola as master of Britain from south coast to north, east coast to west, with only Ireland outside his control. Indeed, he even sends a fleet to circumnavigate the island, an event that seems to be borne out by archaeology in the form of bronze plaques found in York that references one of the sailors.

Yes, I know. Scotland was not Roman. But it *was* conquered by Rome. At the end of AD 83, Agricola could safely claim that Britannia was Roman. The process of Romanisation even seems to have begun. What happened next was, in reality, nobody's fault. Agricola, having served longer than anyone could ever expect on the island, a man now very much one with Britannia, was withdrawn to Rome, having served an extraordinarily lengthy governorship. He there simply retires, suffers increasing ill health, and finally dies with honour and dignity. And while the world continues to damn the emperor Domitian, we cannot lay the blame for the lack of Britain's conquest at his feet. With Britain home to more Roman military than any other province, Domitian was faced with disastrous border incursions in the Balkans. He simply could not afford to maintain the newly won north of Britain, for if he did, he would probably lose the lucrative east. And so, Domitian has the army pull back to Hadrian's Wall and abandon all Agricola's conquests. This must have aggrieved the emperor every bit as much as it would the conqueror himself, but a man in control of an empire has hard decisions to make.

And so the north was won, and then given up before the blood had even cooled. But in all this we must recognise Agricola for what he was and what he achieved. He was the longest serving Roman noble ever to grace the island, he learned its idiosyncrasies, and he used them to complete conquest of Britain. In 7 years he handed the emperor an island entire, and even sent his navy round it and looked at Ireland for an encore.

Why should we know Agricola? Simply because no Roman, in four centuries, had more effect on the course of the province. Dis Manicus, Gnaeus. You are remembered.

Simon Turney is a historian and novelist and author of *Agricola: Architect of Roman Britain*.

The Extraordinary Emperor, by Harry Sidebottom

Heliogabalus, or Elagabalus as he is also known, is an extraordinary figure in Roman history. His short reign was marked by scandal, but he has left his mark on history, and his story is irresistible. Bestselling author and historian Harry Sidebottom examines this complex figure.

A mild Spring night in Syria, 15 May AD218, a small party slips out of the city of Emesa. It is bound for the legionary fortress of Raphanin. The group is headed by Julia Maesa, an elderly Syrian, sister of the late empress Julia Domna. She intends to place her fourteen-year-old grandson on the throne. The journey passes without incident, the gates of the camp swing open. After hours of tense negotiation, at dawn the legionaries proclaim the youth Imperator Marcus Aurelius Antoninus. As far as he is remembered at all in the modern world usually it is as Heliogabalus.

Just under a month later, 8 June, the village of Immae, some twenty-four miles from Antioch. The rebels have two legions now, and some auxiliaries. They face the praetorians and the imperial field army under the emperor Macrinus. The rebellious troops begin to give way. Maesa and her daughter Soaemias leap down from their carriages to try to rally their men. The tide is turned when Heliogabalus draws his sword, and gallops his mount as if to charge the enemy. Losing his nerve, Macrinus flees the battlefield. Against every expectation, Maesa has succeeded; her grandson has become emperor.

It had all started so well. In the next four years everything was to go wrong. They were to be the strangest the Roman empire ever experienced. Heliogabalus humiliated the Senate, promoting low born favourites to high office. Numerous members of the elite were executed. The survivors thought the charges trumped up. Heliogabalus killed his old tutor with his own hand. He paid no attention to the army, and rode roughshod over the interests of the palace staff (the familia *Caesaris*). Although he married at least three women – one, a vestal virgin, to the horror of public opinion, he married twice – he flouted conventional Roman sexuality, flamboyantly boasting of enjoying the passive role in male-male sex, and took the role of the bride in a wedding with a charioteer. It was rumoured he prostituted himself, and asked the imperial physicians about the possibility of a physical sex change. Ignoring the duties of an emperor, he squandered vast amounts of money on entertainments and the worship of his ancestral god Elagabal, which was manifest as a large black stone. His religious zealotry led him to wear oriental priestly garb and enthrone Elagabalus as head of the state pantheon in place of Jupiter Optimus Maximus. The contemporary Cassius Dio later wrote that it was as if the world had been turned upside down. Eventually Heliogabalus was killed by the praetorian guard in another coup orchestrated by his grandmother. Julia Maesa watched her grandson, and one of her daughters, murdered, stripped naked, beheaded, and their corpses dragged with iron hooks. She was not a woman to cross.

The brief reign of Heliogabalus is not only an almost forgotten yet fascinating story, it is also a prism through which we can view some of the most important themes in Roman history: political power, religion, sex, and ethnicity. In the last half century, it has become a scholarly orthodoxy that the role of the emperor was essentially passive; he was not expected to pursue any policies, but merely reacted to the actions of others, mainly petitions from his subjects. Heliogabalus undermines any such modern certainty. His radical restructuring of the state religion was anything but passive. Roman paganism was polytheistic and open to new gods. The opposition to the innovations of Heliogabalus show the limits of such openness. There was nothing intrinsically wrong with introducing eastern deities – Mithras and Jupiter Dolichenus had widespread popularity – or exotic rites; the rituals of Isis were very ostentatiously alien. The problem was not only the emperor swapping the Roman toga for eastern priestly costume and participating in Syrian rituals. More important was his supplanting Jupiter Optimus Maximus with Elagabal. Every pious Roman knew that the safety (*Salus*) of the empire depended on the *Pax Deorum* (probably best translated as the pact with the gods): if the Romans did the right thing by the gods, they would do the right thing by Rome. Placing an eastern black stone above Jupiter threatened the *Pax Deorum*, and thus the Salus, and very existence of Rome.

Roman sexuality was different from that in the modern West. Labels like heterosexual and homosexual do not fit the ancient world; no words in Latin or Greek translate our concepts. For elite males (and we know more about them than any other group, as they wrote the surviving texts) sexual morality in the Classical period was less about the gender of who you had sex with than about being the penetrator or the penetrated. Although there are occasional hints of a counter culture, mainstream morality held that if a male were penetrated even once it left an indelible shame. The lifestyle choices of Heliogabalus were a crucial reason that he was condemned. Often such condemnations sneered at his eastern (Syrian or Phoenician) origins. This raises a live scholarly debate: were the Romans racist? They divided the world into a few simple blocks: northerners were big, pale, drunken, lazy, violent, and so stupid they were incapable of rationality; easterners were smaller, cowardly, cunning, untrustworthy, and superstitious; Africans were much like easterners. If the Romans were less overtly racist than some modern cultures it was because they had another group to fear, demonise, and despise – a group that lived among them, in their own homes – slaves. Romans may not have hated Heliogabalus primarily because he was Syrian, but it made it easier to loath the young emperor.

As far as he is remembered at all in the modern world… Heliogabalus has had a varied afterlife. His memory was condemned in Rome: his statues, and his name on inscriptions, defaced or removed. This *Damnatio Memoriae* did not work. There was always the reminder of the empty space on the plinth, and Classical authors enjoyed castigating him as a tyrant, the worst of all emperors. His memory was forgotten in the Medieval West. When he re-emerged in the Renaissance it was again as a model of tyranny. In the late nineteenth century, he had a strange revival when the Decadent Movement remodelled him as one of their own; a sensual hedonist, who despised conventional bourgeois morality. This was the intellectual background to the famous painting *The Roses of Heliogabalus* by Sir Lawrence Alma-Tadema. All the few subsequent visions of the emperor are filtered through this painting. Nowadays Heliogabalus is confined to the margins. He is still present, among the teetering ziggurats of books and files, in the studies of a few (actually very few) scholars. Now and then he makes a fleeting appearance in the fatuous publicity of fashion houses, and in the discourse of some pretentious art criticism. But there is one afterlife he might have enjoyed. Some on the fringes of the LBGQ+ community have elevated him into a `Queer Icon` or `the first transwoman to rule Rome`. When hailed as emperor by a potential lover, Heliogabalus is meant to have said, `Call me not Lord, for I am a Lady`.

Harry Sidebottom is a bestselling historian and novelist and the author of The Mad Emperor: Heliogabalus and the Decadence of Rome.

Interview: Lucy Worsley on Agatha Christie

Lucy Worsley, historian and broadcaster, has taken on the challenge of writing a new biography of Agatha Christie, the highest selling writer of all. She sat down with us to talk about the Christie, her life and the many screen adaptations.

Lucy, many congratulations on the new book. The subtitle is _An Elusive Woman_, her reported words in an interview in December 1926. Was this a difficult project to embark on, and how do you feel about Christie now you've finished?

I liked Christie before I began, but now I love her. That's warts and all, light and shade! I was worried at first that she would be too successful, too famous, too magnificent, for my readers to really warm to her. There's something a bit prickly and difficult about her public image. But the woman and her image are totally different things. I discovered so many fragilities and vulnerabilities that I ended up feeling almost protective of her. She would in later life present herself as 'the Duchess of Death,' this powerful, enigmatic figure who rarely gave interviews. But that was a way of armouring herself, I believe. It was self-protection. I knew right from the start that I wanted to intertwine her life story with a broader story about the twentieth century. I think her defining feature was her modernity, whether that's big things like being a working mother, exploring psychotherapy, living through two World Wars, being divorced - or little ones, like her passion for speed. In the 1920s, she learned how to surf in Hawaii, and in the 1960s she would drive her car at its maximum velocity of 85 miles an hour down the new M4 motorway. For a girl born in the reign of Queen Victoria, she broke all sorts of rules.

She is the most successful novelist of all time, and a woman – how much of a female icon is she?

An underestimated one! The cliché runs that Agatha Christie has been outsold only by Shakespeare and the Bible – but she achieved that as a woman in a world made by men. With her films playing endlessly on Sunday afternoons, I think that her success came to seem like part of the wallpaper of life – people forget what a ground-breaker she was. But she's not a completely obvious role model, because she never felt able to claim that sort of status for herself. In later life she always talked down the value of her work, describing herself as 'just' a housewife, and would have vehemently denied that she was anything like a feminist. That's partly the values of her upper-middle class Victorian childhood, I think, but it was also, I believe, the legacy of a terrible public shaming she got in the notorious year (we'll come onto this shortly!) of 1926. She ended up hating being a public figure.

Successful as she is, there are some themes in her novels that are problematic today. She was clearly a woman of her time. How do you think we should view Agatha Christie today?

Not just as entertainment. For a historian, her works and her archive present a treasure trove of evidence for the attitudes of a great swathe of Middle England (and beyond) throughout the span of the twentieth century. The attitudes in her work were echoed with her readers. I think as historians we have to study them to see the deep-rooted origins of problems that still affect the world today. But her novels are also interesting as evidence of changing attitudes: there's more same-sex desire, there are more liberal attitudes towards, say, Iraqi people, as the decades go on. And to me it seems lazy to pigeon-hole her, as people tend to, simply as a conservative writer. Her novels operate by presenting you with widely-accepted stereotypes, then sometimes turning them on their heads. Most obviously, never underestimate Hercule Poirot, even if he's a rather camp war refugee who hasn't been to public school. And of course it's perilous to mess with that fluffy little old lady called Miss Marple. I think Christie the writer is basically critical of British culture. She says rottenness is everywhere. People don't seem to realise that she often takes the perspective of an outsider.

She grew up in a wealthy family in Devon during the Edwardian period. How influential was this environment on her, both from a literary standpoint, and her personality?

Agatha's destiny was to follow her older sister into marriage (preferably to a rich man) and motherhood. To that end, her parents hardly educated her - she claimed to have taught herself to read. Her siblings were much older, so she spent a lot of time entertaining herself with the imaginary friends who were the precursors of her literary characters. She was brought up in a leisurely, loving family. But this wasn't necessarily a good preparation for a life that would encompass war, and divorce, and a lack of money.

Her disappearance in 1926 became a huge news story at the time, but she didn't mention it in her 1977 autobiography, published after her death. It would appear on the surface to be a bout of mental illness, what are your thoughts on the episode?

Her Autobiography does mention it! And so do newspaper interviews she gave, particularly a very full one in 1928. But I'm not surprised you think otherwise, and you're not alone! The fact is that Agatha was really quite open about this being a dangerous, distressing episode of mental illness. 'I just wanted my life to end' are the words she uses, of the night she famously 'disappeared'. But journalists at the time, and historians since, haven't really wanted to believe her. That's because it was uncomfortable back then – and it's still uncomfortable now - to hear a woman talking about mental health. That's why the papers at the time instead suggested she might have hidden herself away on purpose, either to seek publicity, or even to frame her cheating husband for her murder. I think if you listen to what she says – rather than to the claims made by male policemen and journalists and the historians who've repeated them – the so-called mystery of her 'disappearance' just melts away.

Christie's novels often involved infidelity, or other kinds of sexual dynamic. Was this due to her first marriage which ended unhappily, and heartbreak?

The cheating husband is certainly a character she would go on to write with great power and conviction. You're right to draw attention to her betrayal by her first husband Archie Christie (who left her for a younger woman) because I think for Agatha it confirmed that even the people closest to you could be false. It made her into the deliciously gothic writer that she became. But it's also fair to say that all her characters, not just the husbands, have a dark secret of one sort or another. Like the cynical Miss Marple herself, Agatha has no illusions.

What's your favourite Agatha Christie novel?

I love *The Murder at the Vicarage* of 1930, Miss Marple's first appearance in a novel. It's so amazingly clever. For much of the book, you don't even realise that this negligible little old lady even is the detective. And I believe that Miss Marple was Agatha's most treasured character, the one who stood for the Agatha herself. They end up growing old together, and use lots of the same tricks for misdirecting our attention away from their formidable brains. Also, that particular book was written as a kind of wedding present to her second, much-loved husband, Max Mallowan, to whom Agatha remained married for forty-five years. Miss Marple is the product of second chance at life and love. I'm happy for Agatha that she got it.

We've seen a resurgence recently with the new Poirot movies starring Kenneth Branagh, and adaptations are often on the small screen. And, of course, The Mousetrap has been running in the West End since 1952. Do you think we'll still be reading/watching Agatha Christie whodunnits in 50 years?

Yes, for two reasons. I think the best of her books stand up to being adapted again and again, for each new generation, like Austen. And then secondly, these whodunnits are such important evidence for how people thought of Britain and Britishness for much of the twentieth century. I argue that you should read Christie not only for pleasure but also to learn about history.

My favourite Poirot is played by Peter Ustinov, but which depiction is the most faithful to the novels?

Ah, I'd say none of them! Agatha herself hated films of her books, and even the great starry thespians who played the part could never quite capture her Poirot to her own satisfaction! And I do think that the screen adaptations tend to compress and water down the brilliance of Christie. Switch off, is what I say, and go back to the books instead.

Lucy Worsley is a historian and broadcaster and author of *Agatha Christie: An Elusive Woman.*

Book Reviews

Act of Oblivion, by Robert Harris

Review by Miranda Malins

In his new historical thriller *Act of Oblivion*, Robert Harris brings his unrivalled ability to create vivid characters within tightly-honed plots to the turbulent Civil Wars and Restoration. It is 1660 and the new King Charles II has just been restored to the throne after eleven years of republican rule. Eager to draw a line under the recent bloody past, the King's new Act of Indemnity and Oblivion promises forgiveness for all who opposed the crown, with one exception: the men responsible for executing his father King Charles I in 1649. They are branded traitors and assigned that most gruesome of retributive deaths; that of hanging, drawing and quartering. While the living (and even some of the dead) are swiftly rounded up and dispatched, a handful of regicides remain at large.

Act of Oblivion focuses on two of these real men, Colonel Edmund Whalley and his son-in-law Colonel William Goffe, as they flee across the Atlantic to the vast remoteness of New England, and their pursuit by an invented government agent Richard Nayler. What follows is an epic manhunt, pitting Whalley and Goffe's arduous, terrifying flight against Nayler's obsession with bringing to justice these Roundheads who he has his own personal reason to hate. The canvass for this cat and mouse chase is huge in time and space yet the tension does not sag. Each time the desperate Whalley and Goffe shut themselves in an attic, barn or Puritan priest hole at the approach of torchlit riders, you can smell the tallow candle smoke and hear their ragged breath in the darkness.

But this is more than a boys' own adventure story. Ever the astute political chronicler, Harris captures the unique blend of providence and pathos in this tortured time historians have called the 'Age of Conscience'. Whalley in particular brings this anxiety to the tale as his long, lonely exile prompts him to question his part in the Civil Wars and faith in God's plan. To stave off boredom he writes memoirs of the life he once led at the heart of the New Model Army and his cousin Oliver Cromwell's Protectorate. This enables Harris to tell the story of these extraordinary times in reflection, and to access the complex mental world of the people caught up in them.

The relationship between the two fugitives lies at the heart of the book and succeeds both in showing the raw, odd intimacy of their shared existence and the fault lines within the Parliamentarian side which ultimately caused its collapse. By the end, after a tense and exciting showdown, we are left with the lingering sense of frustrated sadness which characterised the experience of many Parliamentarians living under the Restoration; their remarkable lives and achievements legislated into oblivion. Why had God asked this of them? What had it all been for? *Act of Oblivion* cannot answer these questions but in Whalley and Goffe's strange love story it shows the terrible price paid by so many for an unknown future.

Miranda Malins is a historian and novelist and author of *The Puritan Princess* and *The Rebel Daughter*.

Devil Dogs: King Company, From Guadalcanal to the Shores of Japan, by Saul David

Review by Justin Doherty

British schoolchildren don't get taught much about the Pacific theatre of World War II, just as the carnage of the Eastern Front gets overlooked in favour of Dunkirk and D-Day. The Pacific war wasn't just strategically significant, it cost the lives of over 100,000 US servicemen and the three years of fighting set the reputation and tone for the US Marines for generations to come. The Japanese invasion of the US territories of Guam, Wake Island, and the Philippines (often considered the worst military defeat in US history), the loss of British Hong Kong, Malaya and Burma, and the subsequent tide-turning Japanese naval defeat at the battle of Midway, set the scene for the long US counterattack across the Pacific. This three-year campaign is the subject of *Devil Dogs*.

Saul David, one of the most prolific and enjoyable narrative military historians of our time, explicitly references Stephen Ambrose's *Band of Brothers* as a template. The narrative follows the men of K Company from the 'first big American offensive of the war', the seizure of the Pacific Island of Guadalcanal, fighting through the islands of New Britain, Peleliu and finally onto Okinawa. In between the men get to spend hard-earned time in Australia and on Pavuvu, enjoying R&R and doing the things off duty Marines are expected to do: drinking and womanising.

Devil Dogs comes alive thanks to the cast of colourful characters as they sleep, eat, fight, and die during these unremittingly challenging combat operations. If you've ever wondered how the US Marines ended up tough and violent, their lasting ethos is surely forged in the jungles of the Pacific where lack of food, malaria and the jungle environment take their toll, the suicidal Japanese fight to the death, surrender is not an option, and uncivilised enemy action commonplace (including targeting medics and prisoners). Camaraderie and fellow Marines are all that's left, "It taught us loyalty to each other - and love. That esprit de corps sustained us."

Many Marines are skin and bone by the time they are relieved from the front line, losing up to a third of their pre-combat body weight. Jolly japes abound such as stealing a turkey, and ordering the men out onto morning parade 12-hours early in a drunken confusion. The author has an instinctive empathy for the ordinary soldier. Poor leadership by inexperienced or flawed officers endangers lives and features often in the men's concerns. One officer threatens his men with court martial for stealing fruit, a crime he himself is guilty of. His sergeant wonders "what kind of officer is this?"

Devil Dogs stands alongside Karl Marlantes' *Matterhorn* for pathos, drama, and insight. David draws upon an array of excellent sources including the US Marine Corps official account, personal memoirs including the respected bestseller (in America) *With the Old Breed* by Eugene Sledge, and Japanese accounts of the war. This is particularly gratifying given Sir Max Hastings' acknowledgment that 'in most Western accounts of the war, the Japanese remain stubbornly opaque.'

Read *Devil Dogs*, and at the very least you'll be transported in ways that history often struggles to. If you're young enough I'll be surprised if you don't have a serious think about visiting the local recruiting office. You have been warned.

Justin Doherty is a security consultant and former army officer.□

Colditz: Prisoners of the Castle, by Ben Macintyre

Review by Oliver Webb-Carter

Colditz had held a fascination for generations of schoolchildren after the Second World War, and I am no different. The POW prison close to Leipzig, in Saxony, was an imposing 16th century castle, and has seen a number of depictions including *The Colditz Story* (1955) starring John Mills, the *TV Series Colditz* (1972), and who can forget the great board game, *Escape from Colditz*? The story is therefore familiar, and who doesn't enjoy tales of daring escapes, whether successful or not, as merciless Nazis brutalise prisoners throughout their confinement? We now have a new history of Colditz Castle during the war, this time told by Ben Macintyre, and it is an intriguing one, because whilst breakouts and Nazis are obviously in here, the story is much more nuanced than the memoirs, movies and TV series, and certainly not what I expected.

One example is class warfare. Naturally, when the British arrive in any part of the world in numbers of more than one, the class structure imposes itself, and Colditz was no different. Not only were officers assigned an orderly, that same orderly was forcibly removed from his POW camp to become a servant for the remainder of the war at the castle. The officers clearly didn't treat these men very well because at one point, militancy set in, a strike resulted, with the rallying cry that they would "only take orders from the Germans!"

One of my personal heroes of the story is Alex Ross, orderly to the hugely famous Douglas Bader, daredevil pilot and fighter ace, and an absolutely terrible human being. Macintyre's depiction is hilarious, and if any man deserved a medal for his wartime service, it was Ross, who had to wait on Bader hand and foot throughout, and for no thanks whatsoever.

Of course, since the prison was all male, homosexuality was a factor that, whilst not directly referred to in the memoirs of inmates, was inevitable, and Macintyre addresses it head on, and with sensitivity. Also written beautifully, are the accounts of mental illness resulting in a number of distressing episodes, in particular that of Frank Flinn who spent much of his time in solitary confinement.

The prisoners' German captors are also not the ogres one expects. Hauptmann Reinhold Eggers is constantly disappointed by the rudeness of his British captives, nothing like the polite and well-mannered Englishmen he encountered on his holidays to the West Country before the war.

The escape attempts from the various nationalities imprisoned at Colditz, inevitably competitively scored, are but one strand of quite a complex tale. One turns the pages at a pace, as is customary from this author, but Macintyre has managed to re-tell a classic Second World War in a fascinating and jaw-dropping account that is sure to be a great success.

Oliver Webb-Carter is the Editor of *Aspects of History*.

Dancing on Bones: History and power in China, Russia and North Korea, by Katie Stallard

Review by David Boyle

I believe it was Talleyrand who described the Bourbons on the grounds that they forget nothing and remember nothing. The same could be said of ancien regimes and ultra-nationalists everywhere – from Northern Ireland to India.

But what the *New Statesman's* senior editor for China and Global Affairs, and former Sky TV reporter, Katie Stallard, does in this compelling and important book is to focus on three extreme versions of this totalitarian approach to history, three authoritarian regimes around the world.

What is so interesting also is what holds them together – Putin's Russia, Xi's China and Kim's North Korea. Because this is no longer an ideological battle – it is far more likely that this is a process that every authoritarian regime has to go through before it can make sure it is safe, whether they are ostensibly left (Xi), or right (Putin).

When the Soviets picked the 'Korean Gandhi', Cho Man-sik as leader of the North, Cho introduced him on the platform at a party rally, where he read a speech written for him by his Soviet masters, called the 'reception for the triumphant return of General Kim Il-sung'. The audience failed to respond to his extravagant praise of the USSR, and they jeered him as a 'fake'.

When Cho was ousted and arrested, the Soviets fell back on Plan B – to weave a story about Kim, helped along by the man himself.

"This was just the beginning," writes Stallard. "Over the next four decades, Kim would continue to exaggerate his accomplishments until he was claiming credit for defeating the Japanese almost single-handedly. His cult of personality would exceed the heights even Stalin's cult reached, and he would build a dynasty that would outlast the USSR. But it all started with the first foundation myth that Kim Il-sung was a guerrilla hero who had played a crucial role in the fight to free his country from colonial rule."

Since 2017, all schools in China need to use the same textbooks for teaching history, Chinese and moral education. Two years later, the new history textbook reduced coverage of the Cultural Revolution to one page and beefed up the coverage of China's current claims on Hong Kong, Taiwan and the South China Sea.

Aleksei Navalny, the courageous opponent of Putin, was forced to watch Russian TV in prison for eight hours a day, and the experience of watching endless rehearsals of the Great Patriotic War was instructive as a way of understanding Putin's strategy: "The present and the future are both substituted with the past – the truly heroic past, or embellished past, or completely fictional past," he wrote.

So how do totalitarian ways of looking at history differ from Conservative ministers getting hot under the collar about the way history is taught here? Or endless political references to the Blitz, which provides the mythology of the modern British state?

Stallard has an answer to that one, which you will have to read the book to discover. But I will say what the title means: the phrase 'dancing on bones' came from a Russian activist who used it to describe the remembrance of history that only serves those now in power.

David Boyle is a historian and writer and author of *Munich 1938: Prelude to War* and *Dunkirk: A Miracle of Deliverance*.

Russia: Myths & Realities, by Rodric Braithwaite

Review by Timothy Ashby

In his new book, *Russia: Myths and Realities*, Rodric Braithwaite, former UK ambassador in Moscow and during the crucial years of 1988-92, takes an eloquent, broad-brush approach to the history of the country described by Churchill as "a riddle, wrapped in a mystery, inside an enigma". Like human beings, Russia as a nation hasn´t changed much over the past thousand years due to the nature of the land and its people, the latter today being driven by the same impulses as their ancestors a millennium ago. Yet Churchill also sagely suggested that "perhaps there is a key" to Russia´s foreign policy and "That key is Russian national interest". Ambassador Braithwaite supports this with historical examples up to the present day, but adds a second key to understanding contemporary Russia – "bloated patriotism".

That bloated patriotism today, which is just one factor in the attempted war of conquest in Ukraine, was born out of deeply wounded national pride after the catastrophic fall of the Soviet Union. I worked in Russia in the 1990s and witnessed first-hand the economic suffering of the Russian people. From my years in St. Petersburg I vividly recall black-clothed old women – many of them war widows - shivering in bleak walkways under boulevards trying to sell pathetic possessions such as worn shoes and chipped crockery. After giving $5.00 to one such person, she followed me for a block, crossing herself and blessing me whist weeping. I was weeping too, in pity for her and the poverty around me.

Fortunately for Braithwaite´s general thesis, the February 2022 invasion of Ukraine took place before his book went to press, providing an opportunity to reflect on Russia´s imperial ambitions. He admits that the judgement, which he had shared, "that the Russians had lost their imperial itch had turned out to be terribly wrong". Putin, he writes, "consumed by his own myth" had condemned his country to widespread ostracism and an indefinite postponement of its chances of becoming ´normal´.

He predicts that Russia can no longer resume its old role as the second superpower, as it has been supplanted by China. Based on Russia´s thousand-year history and national character, I think it would be a mistake to write it off so easily. Despite its autocratic government, Russia today is a dynamic society, with people educated beyond the increasingly "dumbed down" standards of the USA and UK, and the country is aggressively capitalist (I have described modern Russia as "capitalism on steroids"). I agree with Braithwaite that Russians see the West as irredeemably decadent, and they take a long view of history versus our short-termism. Russia will rise again, long after Putin has left the world stage.

Ambassador Braithwaite is a leading Russologist and understands the Russian national character derived from its history. I look forward to his policy advice on how the West can most effectively confront this surly bear that has not shed its dark coat for a lighter one over its history.

Timothy Ashby is a former diplomat, writer and historian and the author of *The Bear in the Back Yard: Moscow's Caribbean Strategy*.

☐

Abyss: The Cuban Missile Crisis 1962, by Max Hastings

Review by Mark Ellis

I have read a good deal about the Kennedys, both generally and in research detail when one of my detective novels featured the family patriarch, Joe, as a character. Joe Kennedy was not a very nice man, and he passed on some of his less pleasant characteristics to his sons. The personal failings of the most famous and glamorous of the clan, John F Kennedy, are well-known and as a politician he always struck me as overrated. This riveting analysis by Max Hastings of the 1962 Cuban Missile Crisis, however, obliges me to reassess. For Kennedy's cool head and careful judgement in dealing with Russia's Cuban adventure might well have been the principal factors which saved the planet from destruction.

The central part of the book is a description of the deliberations and decisions during those famous 13 days in October when the risk of nuclear Armageddon through accident or intent seemed perilously high. He leads us into the meat of his story with a concise evaluation of the state of America, Russia and Cuba in the years immediately prior to the crisis. Among the many interesting new things I learned in this preliminary section was that the first manned space flight by Yuri Gagarin was bedevilled with technical problems and very nearly ended in disaster. This is indicative of the fact that Russia was far less technologically advanced than it liked to pretend.

'I remember thinking the world was going to end any time now' says one American man, a child in 1962, who is quoted by Hastings. I was 9 years of age in 1962. I remember the crisis but don't think I registered the full extent of the danger. I do remember though the palpable sense of unease among the adults in my family. The book sets out in fine detail what a close-run thing everything was and provides fascinating portraits of all the key characters. Kennedy and his team spent much of their time trying to second guess what they thought were complex Russian strategic thought processes when it seems in fact that no deep strategic thinking existed. It seems most likely that the impetus for Khruschev's plan derived from little more than a desire to throw dirt in Kennedy's face with little thought given to the consequences. Thus when Kennedy, ignoring pressure from the US military to invade Cuba, nevertheless acted firmly by setting up a blockade, Khruschev struggled to find an appropriate response. In the end Kennedy remained resolute in negotiation and the Russians backed down. The behaviour of Kennedy's military chiefs, with USAF head Curtis LeMay to the fore, was shockingly cavalier and irresponsible. Stanley Kubrick's classic film *Doctor Strangelove* seems to have been dangerously close to the truth.

One question prompted by this history is why, at a time when Russia has just launched a full-out war on the continent of Europe, the nuclear dangers don't seem to be troubling us in the same way as they did in 1962? Is Putin a much less formidable and more reasonable antagonist than Khruschev? On the evidence of this book and current developments I would think not. Why then the more relaxed attitude to the chances of mutual destruction? I'm not sure I know the answer. Meanwhile Abyss is an excellent book and I highly recommend it.

Mark Ellis is a writer and author of *Dead in the Water.*
  ☐ ☐

Winters in the World: A Journey Through the Anglo-Saxon Year, by Eleanor Parker

Review by M.J. Porter

Winters in the World is an engrossing journey through the Saxon year, using poetry and the writings of the great Saxon scholars to try and determine how time was reckoned and what marked the year for those living in the very weather-dependent agrarian kingdoms of Saxon England. Using the words of the poets and scholars, often anonymous in their current form, Eleanor Parker explains how the Saxon people determined the passage of time, how certain seasons, such as winter, held a particular fascination and perhaps horror, and one that in the surviving written sources is remarkably consistent.

We journey from Winter to Spring, to Summer and then to Autumn, where we learn that the Saxons at one time perhaps only acknowledged two seasons, that of Winter and Summer, before being Christianised. We learn of what the pagan Saxons may have called their months and how the overlaying of a Christian calendar was a deliberate attempt to bring into some sort of agreement the calendar of the Mediterranean of the Bible with the much more seasonal weather of England.

What I loved about this book were all the translations of the poems and religious writings, the Old English words are often given, and their translation so that readers can try and decipher one from the other. Often in books such as these, there's an expectation that the reader can understand the sources, which can be very frustrating. Knowing the names of the scholars Ælfric of Eynsham and Byrhtferth of Ramsey, it was wonderful to see their words woven into the narrative in a way that brought their writings to life as more than just men who wrote the lives of saints.

It's interesting to know that the Saxon people were as preoccupied with winter and its beauty as we might be, and equally, that the seasons could be used as a metaphor for the lives of men and women, just as we still do. There are many poems and sources with religious preoccupations, and it's fascinating to learn about the ancient celebrations and traditions, how words have come to define seasons, and finally, know what Rogationtide was all about. Eleanor Parker reveals how these religious festivities were used to mark the passage of time in the Anglo-Saxon Chronicles and, in doing so, adds a whole new dimension to one of my favourite sources from the period.

This is a beautifully evoked story of the Saxons and the way they reckoned time, and Eleanor Parker is keen to explain the religious significance of many of the events and, more importantly, how they might have changed over time and yet still very much define many of the public holidays and festivals that occur within England today. For any who might fear delving into poetry and sermons, I can assure you that this book is told with an engaging and light touch. It is simply fascinating.

M.J.Porter is a bestselling novelist and author of *The Son of Mercia*.

Shadow of the Tower, by Peter Tonkin

Review by Emily Ronald

The second book in the Queen's Intelligencer series from Peter Tonkin, *Shadow of the Tower* sees familiar characters return for more intrigue, more plots, and more twists.

Although set two years after the previous novel which was centred around the famous Essex rebellion, our story here opens in 1570 with James Stewart, 1st Earl of Moray, walking through Linlithgow on a cold winter morning. 'The Gude Regent', as he is known, has great plans for the kingdom of Scotland, and for the Protestant church. However, these are cut short when he is assassinated, quite gruesomely, by supporters of the Catholic Queen Mary.

We then fast-forward to 1600: thirty years have passed, and the Earl of Moray's young charge, James VI, is now a man fully grown, able to make his own decisions - and his own enemies. He is lured to Gowrie house by the Ruthven brothers on the promise of foreign gold, but the only thing waiting for the king is a knife wielded in revenge. Once more the reader discovers the perils of ruling; the Ruthvens discover the peril of attempting regicide, meeting a bloody end.

Three years later, the great Queen Elizabeth I lies dying, her court waiting with bated breath for her to name her successor. To Secretary of State Robert Cecil, the line of succession to James VI is clear. The trouble will be in keeping him alive long enough to be coronated.

Foremost of his spies is, of course, Robert Poley, who must uncover plot after plot from ambitious magnates and clergymen while the new king journeys to London from Edinburgh to take the throne.

The true talent of any historical fiction author is to take the complex web of events from hundreds of years ago and tie them together into a gripping plot that excites the audiences of today. This is exactly what Peter Tonkin achieves, creating a plot so gripping that readers are left excited to turn the page and see how he ends it, even if they know what the actual outcome of the events was.

The characters that Tonkin creates are so believable and well-researched that readers could be forgiven for believing his versions of them are what they must have truly been like. Of course, there is a wee bit of creative licence used, but this is necessary to make characters long dead come alive again. This is especially true of Robert Poley, who Tonkin truly does justice to. Incredibly cunning and sharp, Poley's ruthlessness as an intelligence is rounded out by his deep emotions and awareness of his flaws, giving his character the human feel that is often lost in history texts.

Like every good historical fiction novel, *Shadow of the Tower* also doesn't assume that every reader has a degree in history, and takes time to explain and give context to relevant events. Besides being helpful, this builds up the layers and drama of the story, leading to an explosive ending that readers will definitely remember.

Emily Ronald is an Editorial Assistant at *Aspects of History.*□

King of the World: Cyrus the Great, by Matt Waters

Review by Luke Pepera

In his preface, Matt Waters mentions that, because evidence concerning the life and achievements of Cyrus the Great, the pre-eminent founder of the Achaemenid Persian Empire, are somewhat lacking, works on and about Cyrus are few and far between. In many ways, this historical biography, a synthesis of Waters' articles and books covering the great ruler previously written, seeks to go some way in addressing this.

Following his discussion of Cyrus' early life, Waters explains how, when Cyrus became king of Anshan in 559 BC, he built up, probably through a series of diplomatic marriages to the offspring of other Iranian peoples who then supported him, his power base. Special treatment is given to the Egyptian princess Cassandane whom, it seems, became at some point Cyrus' main wife, and was particularly crucial to this phase of his life and rule. Then, we get a record of Cyrus' major conquests, beginning with that of the Medes, who in the early-to-mid sixth century were one of the biggest players in the region. After defeating the last Median king, Astyages, and conquering his kingdom in 550BC, Cyrus became the Medians' king, and married Astyages' daughter, Amytis. Having in this way brought the Medes – which, Waters tells us, was a kind of confederation in which a Median overlord dominated multiple, neighbouring peoples who swore allegiance to him – under his control, Cyrus added to his burgeoning empire most of the peoples of northern Iran, including the Hyrcanians, Parthians, Scythians, and Bactrians. In the 540s, after spending some time consolidating his recent conquests, Cyrus subdued the kingdom of Urartu in eastern Anatolia, before vanquishing Croesus and conquering Lydia and the Greek cities he controlled. Next comes Babylon, the premier power of the region at this time, which Cyrus brings under his heel in 539BC.

Even before that last conquest, Cyrus ruled the largest empire that had ever existed up to that point. Waters does well in describing the magnitude of this achievement. He then moves to discuss Cyrus' royal inscriptions from Babylonia, including the all-important so-called Cyrus Cylinder, from which we learn important things about their issuer. To those who might wonder how on earth such an expansive collection of territories in which lived numerous, diverse people was managed, Waters has you covered with an explanation of the tools Cyrus used to organise and govern his realm. A distinctive royal ideology, in whose formation and exercise, Waters stresses, Cyrus consciously assumed and utilised Assyrian concepts, was among the most important of these.

Where else to end but with Cyrus' legacy? After a mention of his death in 530BC, here is considered his reputation among, and impact on, not just his Achaemenid successors, but also the Greeks, whose writers considered him to have been in many ways an exemplary leader. They helped establish and spread a positive image, and Alexander the Great venerated his memory and copied some of his customs, as did the Romans. In sum, this is a fascinating, and, more so, educational work, about a ruler who Waters (arguably rightly) believes should be up there with Alexander the Great, Julius Caesar, and Gengis Khan.

Luke Pepera is a writer, broadcaster and historian, currently working on his first book, *Motherland: 500,000 Years of African History, Cultures, and Identity.* □

Crassus: The First Tycoon, by Peter Stothard

Review by Peter Hughes

Plutarch observed that the "many virtues" of the Roman general and triumvir Marcus Licinius Crassus "were obscured by one vice, avarice." Peter Stothard's life of Crassus is the story of that vice. The book opens by laying bare the contradiction at the heart of the one of the wealthiest men of the ancient world: "The first tycoon of Ancient Rome was also its most famous loser." What follows is the unravelling of this contradiction, as Crassus moves, inexorably, from the pinnacle of power to his ignominious beheading in the Parthian desert.

Stothard exposes the flaws and the genius in the psychology of Crassus after he defeated the slave revolt led by Spartacus. He marched the survivors of Spartacus's army along the Appian Way, the busiest road in Italy, stopping every thirty yards to crucify the last man. It was an ostentatious display of power that was, according to Stothard, "an unprecedented act, requiring power of organisation as well as brutal cruelty, perfectly characterising Crassus." These crucifixions showed Crassus as a cold calculating machine and this quality, combined with his opportunism, defined the business dealings through which he acquired his vast fortune. Wherever fires broke out in Rome, he offered to buy nearby houses at a heavily discounted price, leading Plutarch to comment that "public calamities were his principal source of revenue".

If Crassus had been nothing but a "calculating machine", he might have lived to die of old age, but his drive to acquire more, his pride and overconfidence, led to his death. As a young man he had watched his father and brother killed by a Marian mob, their heads displayed on pikes. In 53 BCE, he saw his son Publius suffer the same fate after Crassus ignored all warnings and omens and pursued a Parthian army into the desert. Shortly after his son's death, Crassus himself was captured, killed and beheaded.

Crassus's dead mouth was forced open and molten gold poured down his throat. In a passage in The Interpretation of Dreams, Sigmund Freud saw this as the fulfilment of an unconscious wish and imagined the Parthian queen (in fact, it was a king!) saying, as the gold was poured, "Now you have what you wanted." After this violation, the head of Crassus was presented to King Orodes II as he watched a performance of the Greek tragedy The Bacchae, a play about the fate of King Pentheus, who was ripped to shreds for his defiance of the god Dionysus. As the play reached its conclusion, the Parthian general Silaces threw the head of Crassus onto the stage where it was used as a prop.

Early in the tragedy, the blind prophet Tiresias warns Pentheus: "You are mad, grievously mad, beyond the power of any drugs to cure, for you are drugged with madness." The madness of Crassus, the fatal contradiction between the cold, calculating tycoon and the unconscious forces that drive him to his death, is also the eternally recurring madness of money, ambition and power that Stothard captures brilliantly in this riveting book.

Peter Hughes is a philosopher, psychologist and historian and author of *A History of Love and Hate in 21 Statues.*□

Agricola, by Simon Turney

Review by Peter Tonkin

I first encountered Agricola in Tacitus during Latin lessons; then in Shipway's Imperial Governor riding against Boudicca's Icenii, as tribune to Legia II Augusta under Paulinus (as Tacitus himself was later to be tribune, possibly to the same legion, and son-in-law under Agricola). I came across him in the South of France, holidaying near Frejus where he was born. Elliott's Roman Britain's Missing Legion – features Agricola as well, because the IXth Hispania may well have gone missing under his governorship. It is a great pleasure to review Simon Turney's brilliant and illuminating Agricola: Architect of Roman Britain.

Turney starts with Tacitus' De vita et moribus Iulii Agricolae which may be translated as 'Of the life and thoughts of Julius Agricola', although 'moribus' is often rendered as 'morals.' I offer this as an example of Turney's technique – time and again he turns to standard translations of Tacitus, balancing one against the other, looking for telling differences in emphasis and occasionally offering his own erudite suggestions.

But Turney is no pedant. Just as he pits one translation against another, so he tests the annals of Agricola's career against the evidence on the ground. As he himself says (P196) '…the application of archaeology and geography to the text of Tacitus is what this is all about.' In so-doing, he finds revealing patterns in night-camps and fortlets which have too often been dismissed. As well as examining Agricola, he revisits the reputations of previous governors such as the influential Scapula (whose impressive conquests Agricola apparently wished to emulate), Paulinus (though he skips over his campaigns against Druidic Wales and Boudicca), Cerialis (who is joined by Agricola in 71(?) as Legate of LegioXX) both recalled in 73 and replaced by the underestimated Frontinus, whom Agricola himself relieved in Summer 77.

Turney's work on the ground – as presented in fascinating detail with maps, lists and photographs of the most important areas - presents us with a pattern of conquest and Romanisation as governor after governor, occasionally with Agricola's help, expands and consolidates Roman Britain, laying foundations upon which Agricola will build. Building, of course, his camps, his forts, his cities, most of which, if not created, are strongly improved by him. This is all, Turney suggests, part of a plan which came to fruition under the Flavians.

The administrations of Flavian emperors, together with other events such as the eruption of Vesuvius (79AD) and the deaths of his sons, all impact upon Agricola's governorship –

causing conquest to pause. But that seemingly allowed the tribes in unconquered Caledonia to get together and plan an attack which came in 82, effectively beginning with the near annihilation of the understrength IX Hispania. This restlessness appears to have prompted Agricola to winter in Scotland (82/3AD despite the loss of his second son) and to use the next fighting season to force the highland tribes into one last, fatal, pitched battle at Mons Graupius (Sept 83AD), completing the conquest of Britannia before Agricola finally retired to Rome and carefully orchestrated, well-earned, obscurity.

Peter Tonkin is a writer and author of The Shadow of the Tower and his latest novels set in ancient Rome, Caesar's Spies.

The Mad Emperor: Heliogabalus and the Decadence of Rome, by Harry Sidebottom

Review by David Boyle

If you were ever interested in Roman decadence – and judging by the number of novels being written set in the ancient city, that probably means a lot of us - then this book really takes the biscuit. I've never encountered Harry Sidebottom before – he teaches ancient history at Lincoln College, Oxford – but I imagine his tutorials or his lectures are a little like this text – clear, compelling and opinionated.

He doesn't just tell the story of this particular ruler – Heliogabalus was a 14-year-old boy who became emperor unexpectedly after intervening in one of Rome's inevitable civil wars – he also tells the academic story about how we know what we know, his opinion on the sources and where he has changed his mind. For someone like me, I have become sceptical of the Roman sources, and the horrible lack on Britannia.

Reading *The Mad Emperor* makes you realise that there is more to it than that. We are as uncertain of Heliogabalus' parentage as he was himself, though he was the cousin of the emperor Caracella. I was convinced by his book that Heliogabalus was a real person, and that he really did drive a chariot pulled by naked women, while he was naked himself, wearing only a large erection. Heliogabalus wasn't actually his name but a description of the sun god he served as priest of his temple based in Emesa in the Syrian province.

What I'm less sure about is whether this 'mad emperor' was really insane. Sex obsessed he may have been, but he was never made his horse a consul, like Caligula – who really was mad. Yes, he played tricks on people, let out wild animals during dinners, married a vestal virgin – twice – became obsessed with men with massive penises and may have become a prostitute. Or that's what the sources say.

"A mule-driver, a courier, a cook…and a locksmith: all appointed to collect the 5% tax on inheritance because of the enormous size of their cocks," writes Sidebottom. "If only the mule-driver and his companions were real, Heliogabalus would have headed the only regime in history that could be called a *phallocracy*."

The army never forgave Heliogabalus for his effeminacy, or for asking surgeons if it was possible to turn him into a woman. He was killed by the Praetorian guard in 222AD, after reigning barely four years – replaced by his even younger cousin Marcianus.

Sidebottom uses the peculiar life of Heliogabalus to look at recent issues in ancient history – which makes the book something of a tour de force, and I particularly enjoyed his attack on historical positivists in the final few paragraphs of his book.

Pretending that history is just "the rhetoric of historians is lazy, arrogant and unimaginative," says Sidebottom in the final phrase of the book. "The past was another country, but it is worth making the effort to imagine how they did things there."

David Boyle is a historian and novelist and author of *Nor Shall My Sword Sleep*, his novel of Caractacus, the Briton who defied the Roman Empire..

Agatha Christie: An Elusive Woman, by Lucy Worsley.

Review by J.C. Briggs

Agatha Christie certainly is in Lucy Worsley's wide-ranging and engaging biography of the Queen of Crime. The heavy-set, bespectacled middle-aged woman of the familiar photographs emerges at as the 'man-magnet' Edwardian beauty who receives nine proposals of marriage. Worsley trains her curator's eye on illuminating detail: the yellow satin worn in Cairo, the surfer in pearls, the World War I nurse taking an amputated leg to be burnt, the pharmacist whose colleague mixed suppositories with a dangerous drug, the intrepid traveller stuck in the desert sand, the serial house buyer, the cream lover. The dedicated writer, of course, and the woman who disappeared – the search for a possible body featuring Dorothy Sayers and Conan Doyle.

Lucy Worsley presents Agatha through the prism of women's lives in the twentieth century. Agatha is an upper middle-class girl, destined for a 'good' marriage – not murder, but her father's death, the loss of their fortune, and the First World War change all that. She makes a career in pharmacy and marries Archie Christie, a dashing pilot, whose background is somewhat rackety – his father had died in a lunatic asylum from the effects of syphilis. The marriage ends in divorce – not expected for that Edwardian beauty. As a single mother, she marries again, very happily, but 'she made herself', Worsley argues, for she was independent, strong-minded, and quite prepared to challenge exploitative publishers.

Several chapters are devoted to that notorious disappearance which Lucy Worsley sees as a defining event in Agatha's writing life. The mystery is a fascinating read, but Agatha was treated appallingly by the press, accused of staging the vanishing to get publicity, and, worse, to wreak revenge on the adulterous Archie, who was suspected of Agatha's murder. Worsley makes a compelling and intriguing case in defence of Agatha. Most importantly, Worsley contends that the humiliation, the exposure, and the psychotherapy treatment enriched her as a writer, deepening the darker elements and focusing her attention on the mind of the murderer. Difficult times, argues Worsley, are creative times for the writer.

Throughout, Worsley carefully links the events and changes in Agatha's life to her work, focusing on her preoccupation with the home in which secrets and horror lie behind the respectable façade. Even as a child, Agatha knew that; she was haunted by a figure she named the Gun Man, a terrifying apparition who becomes in the books the secret murderer of the home.

Lucy Worsley ends by exploring the new critical appraisals of the woman who did not think of herself as an author. Critical studies claim her as a 'modernist' alert to changing times; not a 'conformist', but a novelist 'engaged in reworking the conventional forms of Victorian transgression.'

Whatever the critics think, Agatha Christie's legacy is incontestable, and her biographer celebrates that in this sympathetic, thoughtful, and readable account, which is not, by the way, afraid to tackle the aspects of Christie's work which trouble modern readers and to interrogate the woman writer's difficult relationship with her only child.

J.C. Briggs is a historical crime fiction novelist and author of the *Charles Dickens Investigations*.

☐

Next Issue

Simon Sebag Montefiore on A Family History of the World

Tessa Dunlop on Elizabeth & Philip

Roger Moorhouse on the Nazi-Soviet Pact

Nicola Cornick on Robert Catesby

Printed in Great Britain
by Amazon

15082098R00068